Anti-Racist Practice in the Early Years

A Holistic Framework for the Wellbeing of All Children

Valerie Daniel

Routledge
Taylor & Francis Group

LONDON AND NEW YORK

Designed cover image: Sara, age 3, her 'happy place' is family and sunshine

First published 2023
by Routledge
4 Park Square, Milton Park, Abingdon, Oxon OX14 4RN

and by Routledge
605 Third Avenue, New York, NY 10158

Routledge is an imprint of the Taylor & Francis Group, an informa business

British Library Cataloguing-in-Publication Data
A catalogue record for this book is available from the British Library

Library of Congress Cataloging-in-Publication Data
Names: Daniel, Valerie, author.
Title: Anti-racist practice in the early years : a holistic framework for the wellbeing of all children / Valerie Daniel.
Description: Abingdon, Oxon ; New York, NY : Routledge, 2023. | Series: Little minds matter ; 10 | Includes bibliographical references and index. | Summary: Provided by publisher.
Identifiers: LCCN 2022047715 (print) | LCCN 2022047716 (ebook) | ISBN 9781032162645 (hardback) | ISBN 9781032162652 (paperback) | ISBN 9781003247807 (ebook)
Subjects: LCSH: Early childhood education--Social aspects. | Classroom environment--Social aspects. | Holistic education. | Anti-racism.
Classification: LCC LB1139.23 .D347 2023 (print) | LCC LB1139.23 (ebook) | DDC 372.21--dc23/eng/20221130
LC record available at https://lccn.loc.gov/2022047715
LC ebook record available at https://lccn.loc.gov/2022047716

ISBN: 978-1-032-16264-5 (hbk)
ISBN: 978-1-032-16265-2 (pbk)
ISBN: 978-1-003-24780-7 (ebk)

DOI: 10.4324/9781003247807

Typeset in Optima
by Deanta Global Publishing Services, Chennai, India

"Dr Valerie Daniel is a shining light for our sector. A must-read fo early years professionals and those training to enter into the early ye sector. The way in which Valerie has written this book, firstly, spe from the heart and, secondly, takes you on a journey, one in whi you feel engrossed to continue to read, learn, and reflect on why an racism is an important aspect which truly needs embedding into ou practices."

Aaron Bradbury, *Principal Lecturer – Early Childhood and Childhood, Nottingham Trent University*

"Dr Valerie Daniel introduces her book on anti-racist practice as 'a journey we can walk together' and she delivers. Unafraid to challenge the reader, she does so with compassion. Her warmth, wisdom, and passion for equity in educational settings shine through the text creating the safe space needed for anti-racist reflection and action to take place. Dr Valerie draws upon personal insight and diverse sources to create something unique and refreshing in educational theory."

Alice Ndiaye, *Local Authority Inclusion Adviser*

"Dr Daniel presents a real depth of understanding in this book. She opens up her thoughts, skills, and experiences as an informative guide, highlighting issues of race and anti-racism. Her animation infused and contextualised approach to the complexity of race and racism within the early years features her proficiency to untangle and decipher a convoluted moment in time. The book engages the reader by balancing the uncomfortable with a rich lived experience. The need to effectively become changemakers is a powerful call for all of us to action as reflective practitioners."

Sharon Curtis, *CEO, Emosi – Transcultural Therapeutic Care (TTC)*

Anti-Racist Practice in the Early Years

Are all children treated equally in your class? Are you aware if you are displaying unconscious bias? How might this be playing out in your setting? These conversations need to take place if we are ever to shift systemic racism, for the wellbeing of all children in the early years and beyond.

This essential guide addresses diversity and inclusion in a meaningful and constructive way. The holistic approach explores a range of pertinent topics for the early years and demonstrates the positive impact educators can make by developing their knowledge of systemic racism, critically reflecting upon their provision, and embedding anti-racist practice within their settings.

This book includes:

- A framework to embed and sustain anti-racist practice in early years education.

- Case studies to explore constructions of racism in early childhood and the experiences of black children and their families.

- Reflective questions to encourage readers to consider their own practices and to drive change.

- A brief history of racism to create a sense of understanding and awareness of how we got to where we are today.

- Practical strategies to equip those who work in the early years and to gain confidence in their anti-racist practice.

- A focus on the power of professional love and co-creation to shift the dynamic and build the best outcomes for all children.

By making anti-racism real in our learning environments and reflecting upon and reviewing provision, early years educators can ensure they are committed to their remit of advocacy for the children and communities whose lives they touch. This powerful book is a vital read for all trainee and practising early years professionals, reception teachers, nursery teachers, and managers.

Valerie Daniel is a qualified teacher with over 30 years' experience, with the last 14 years in the role of a Maintained Nursery School headteacher. Valerie is a Doctor of Education, a trained systems leader, and leadership mentor for other headteachers and leaders in the Early Years Sector. She can be found on twitter @Valerie_JKD.

Little Minds Matter

Promoting Social and Emotional Wellbeing in the Early Years

Series Advisor: Sonia Mainstone-Cotton

The *Little Minds Matter* series promotes best practice for integrating social and emotional health and wellbeing into the early years setting. It introduces practitioners to a wealth of activities and resources to support them in each key area: from providing access to ideas for unstructured, imaginative outdoor play; activities to create a sense of belonging and form positive identities; and, importantly, strategies to encourage early years professionals to create a workplace that positively contributes to their own wellbeing, as well as the quality of their provision. The *Little Minds Matter* series ensures that practitioners have the tools they need to support every child.

Supporting Behaviour and Emotions in the Early Years
Strategies and Ideas for Early Years Educators
Tamsin Grimmer

A Guide to Mental Health for Early Years Educators
Putting Wellbeing at the Heart of Your Philosophy and Practice
Kate Moxley

Supporting the Wellbeing of Children with EAL
Essential Ideas for Practice and Reflection
Liam Murphy

Building Positive Relationships in the Early Years
Conversations to Empower Children, Professionals, Families and Communities
Sonia Mainstone-Cotton and Jamel Carly Campbell

Developing Child-Centred Practice for Safeguarding and Child Protection
Strategies for Every Early Years Setting
Rachel Buckler

Little Brains Matter
A Practical Guide to Brain Development and Neuroscience in Early Childhood
Debbie Garvey

Creativity and Wellbeing in the Early Years
Practical Ideas and Activities for Young Children
Sonia Mainstone-Cotton

Anti-Racist Practice in the Early Years
A Holistic Framework for the Wellbeing of All Children
Valerie Daniel

Contents

Trigger warning

Racism is a difficult topic at the best of times. It touches all of our lives in some shape or form and as such it may trigger feelings about the children you work with or create strong emotions regarding your personal situation. This book explores themes on generational trauma and identity-based issues and I would encourage you to note how you are feeling when reading the book and to take care of your mental safety and wellbeing. Be kind to yourself, take a moment to process in the best way you can. Creating a safe space to explore your thoughts, beliefs, values and feelings is a strategy that is explored throughout this book. Remember, your wellbeing is important as it supports your ability to give your best to the children in your care.

Preface

Lately it seems that we can't escape news about racism and all the ways that life is not fair for some people. It is everywhere! Personally, I am exhausted, and more than ready for change. I am well aware that beating the racism drum is not going to magically open the hearts and minds of people, especially those who cannot relate (or don't want to relate) to the experiences of others. Trying to make the point that racism is deeply ensconced in the fabric of UK society is exhausting and I am willing to bet that both you and I are engorged from a well-publicised and not so subtly politicised diet of narratives that only serve to further widen the ideological gulf that we currently find ourselves in. The problem with an ideological gulf is that we are already at the point of "them" and "us": a battleground for winners or losers with very little hope of compromise. This kind of polarisation is emotional and identity-driven and generally keeps us busy with what we believe rather than what we know. We live in a world where divisiveness keeps the wheels of the media in perpetual motion, amplifying extreme views and moral outrage, reducing the lives and experiences of people who suffer racism to a bit of entertainment, especially on social media, when those who desire, can say their worst from a secure hiding place behind their computer screens. This ideological gulf, whether real or virtual, stops normal, everyday people from connecting and forming more accurate impressions of people they perceive to be different to them.

My intention for this book is to engage in a "getting to know each other" process and to offer a literary olive branch (so to speak) for when our ideas and opinions do not appear to align at face value. I will try to avoid sweeping generalisations or a "holier than thou" attitude and more than anything, I will aim to avoid any form of pressure. However, because of the sensitive nature of the subject, I cannot promise that there won't be times when it may feel a bit uncomfortable, but I hope this is a journey we can walk together and when we get to the inevitable crossroads, we can use each other's experiences to choose the path we will take towards a better world for the youngest in our society. So, onwards with this journey. I am excited! I love me a good road trip, especially one where we are going on a driving holiday with a large group of friends and family. Driving in convoy is an interesting experience at the best of times; nevertheless, I still hope that you are as excited as I am. As you know, we have to prepare really well for a road trip, especially a road trip with little ones; so, bring snacks, games, iPads and earphones, juice, plenty of water, travel playlist, podcasts; plan in the toilet breaks but remember to also be ready for the randomness of dealing with little ones who do not subscribe to our best-laid plans. Double-check the route, but if you are in my car, go with the mindset that getting lost is part of the adventure; I am hopeless with directions so without a doubt, I will need your help with the map. OK! The cars are loaded with all the baggage (we are going to need that); as it's a long journey, let's fill up now, but we will definitely need to stop for petrol along the way. Make sure again that everyone is seated as comfortably as is possible in a packed car; buckle up and let's go!

The travel pack

Orientation

Let me start plainly and simply with an introduction. I would like you to meet *me*, Valerie Daniel, free of the expected stereotypical connotations: woke narratives, Black Lives Matter mantras, black woman tropes, everything you think you know about me because I happen to be black. Just one human being to another. I am a 62-year-old Jamaican woman who was a frequent visitor to England when I was younger; I used to come for holidays to visit my family who lived here. After qualifying as a teacher in Jamaica, I came to England to pursue further studies at the grand age of 29 years old and stayed on to live here after meeting my husband. Thankfully, I was able to navigate the system without being burdened by the "baggage" that comes from grow-ing up in a country where the legacy of racism is such a foundational feature that it has almost ceased to be perceptible in everyday life by those who benefit from it, and also where it has become a natural unspoken occurrence that some members of society are expected to do twice as much to only achieve half of their full potential. This phenomenon is a feature of most countries that are classed as "first world" and have multi-culturalism as a societal feature. I want to offer you this: I came here with the privilege of high expectations from my parents and my teachers throughout my educational pursuits, high self-esteem, a fairly uncomplicated value system that was designed for me to reach my full potential, and also as a product of the Jamaican national motto "Out of many, one people," which is a tribute to the unity of the different cultural heritages that coexist in one little island in the Caribbean. It would be untrue to say that as an island we escaped the nuances of "colourism" and "shadeism," (any countries affected by colonial rule will have elements of this) but suffice it to say that racism hits differently in a system where all of us identify as Jamaican and none of us feel like an unwanted guest in the place we call home. I didn't realise how privileged I was until I got here, relatively free of intergenerational trauma, financially independent, and fortified with more than enough emotional reserves and yet, I am still affected in many ways – but that is a story for another time.

Situation

Thirty-two years down the line and a whole lot wiser, I have been able to condense my experiences into a set of personal values that I have used to help to sustain my family. That being said, I still want to wake up in a country where my skin colour is noticed but not noted; where my social standing is not marred by the colour of my skin, and where academic and vocational ability is not so intertwined with racial perceptions that my qualifications are constantly greeted with surprise or disbelief. I want to exist in a space where parenting does not entail preparing my children and grandchildren for the invasion they will encounter into their private lives purely from day-to-day living – walking to school, going into a shop, socialising with friends outdoors. I want to not have to explain that what is viewed as the natural exuberance of youth and a rite of passage for their white friends will not be viewed in the same way for them. I want to avoid the sadness of preparing them for baseless stop and searches and how to survive these traumatic events, all whilst maintaining an air of decorum and a semblance of personal dignity. You might say: if this is your experience of the UK, why don't you just leave? Well, the lives of black and white people have been inextricably interwoven for centuries and leaving does not fix the problem. The systemic reformation I am proposing is centred around the needs of the early years sector, but as we cannot escape the intricacy of systemic racism, it is best to acknowledge this phenomenon at this juncture to set the stage for the proposed changes.

Mission

One of my aims for this book is to explore whether we have approached reading it with some degree of open-mindedness or whether we are holding on to preconceived ideas that are already set in stone in our minds. We know that most of us forget what we have read quite soon after reading it, especially if we fail to find common ground with the author. As the author, I consider it a privilege to have a platform to connect with anyone who reads this book and my deepest wish, is that it is also experienced with others. Unpicked, bashed about, questioned, explored, agreed and disagreed with, revisited time and time again until it is dog-eared and well-worn with evidence of unfamiliar words and phrases that have been circled to be looked up for further definition and with complex ideas that have been highlighted for discussion. We know, as early years practitioners, that learning and engagement sits at the base of change and for us to grasp and hold on to the meaning of things to implement change we have to be "hands on". I hope practitioners who read this book will seek me out and grace me with photos of their well-worn, dog-eared books – that would be the ultimate compliment.

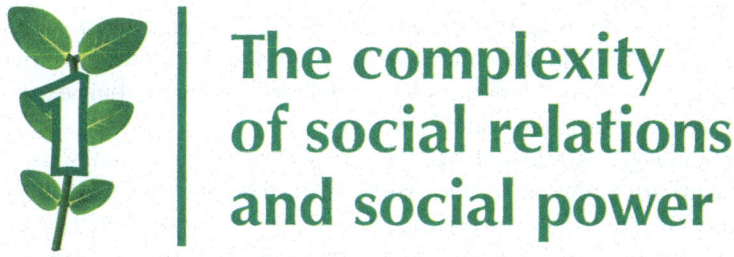

The complexity of social relations and social power

One drop in the ocean can ripple into a wave

"A fish is swimming along one day when another fish comes up and says 'Hey, how's the water?' The first fish stares back blankly at the second fish and then says 'What's water?'" (Kania et al., 2018, p. 2). This little tale reminds us that we all live in the same world but how we experience the world is very, very different. Many of us take the circumstances we live in for granted and are totally unaware of what the world is like for other people because we are so ensconced in our own reality. How we think affects how we live in this world and what we choose to give our attention to, so to be able to alter the lenses through which we see the world, we have to pay attention to how we construct meaning from our experiences. Those of us who work in early years education have a good understanding of the importance of how constructing meaning from experience acts as a powerful tool for learning for young children, who automatically use their experiences to make meaning of the world; but as adults we can also choose to see the world through the eyes of others.

Look at it like this: if the world was a beach (I guess there is no hiding that I am an island girl), we would all, ideally, pay attention to the water we swim in and, hopefully, be mindful of ensuring that we all become competent swimmers, especially our little ones. We would all aim to have a basic level of proficiency in knowing how to help someone who has, for example, been stung by a jellyfish. We would also look to our lifeguards for added assurance. Are they sitting up high enough to have a good vantage point? Are they paying attention to ensure that everyone is safe from harm? Are

DOI: 10.4324/9781003247807-1

they trained well enough to be able to confidently and comfortably deal with anyone who is in difficulty? We are all swimming in this vast ocean of race relations: some people are doing well and enjoying their experience, while others are struggling and drowning.

This analogy is relevant because it presents us all equally as human beings who are partaking in this experience called life. The crucial question is: if you were actually in the ocean and the person next to you, who happened to have a different skin colour to your own, was struggling, would you let them drown? Remember, you could easily be the person who is drowning, because the ocean is no respecter of persons! I don't think many of us would let another person drown, no matter who they are; so, hopefully, the takeaway from this book is to actively think of people who are different from us as being beside us in the ocean and to remember that we are all here to help humanity to thrive.

Racism is a problem that has a number of different but related parts; understanding it as an issue is not easy, let alone finding a neat, single solution that will tackle its complexity to everyone's satisfaction. Kania et al. (2018) explain that complex problems are hard to shift because of the variety of factors that feed into them. They mention factors such as "government policies, societal norms and goals, market forces, incentives, power imbalances, knowledge gaps, embedded social narratives" that compound any complex problem; these factors, and many more, also speak to the complexity of anti-racist practice in the early years. They suggest that "changemakers" need to understand what they are dealing with by identifying all the factors that touch the issue they seek to address and then committing to explore how these factors interact with power dynamics, the culture within our different institutions, and operational constraints as they apply to the issue.

I like the concept of a "changemaker": a changemaker is not a "do-gooder"; a changemaker is passionate about the greater good, taking creative action to work through social problems while inspiring others to change. We all have young changemakers in our early years settings, you know: the child who stands up for another child when they are not being treated fairly, the child who will come to enlist the help of an adult to put a stop to unfair treatment. That three-year-old has empathy, courage, and motivation to make change happen. They haven't carried out a problem analysis,

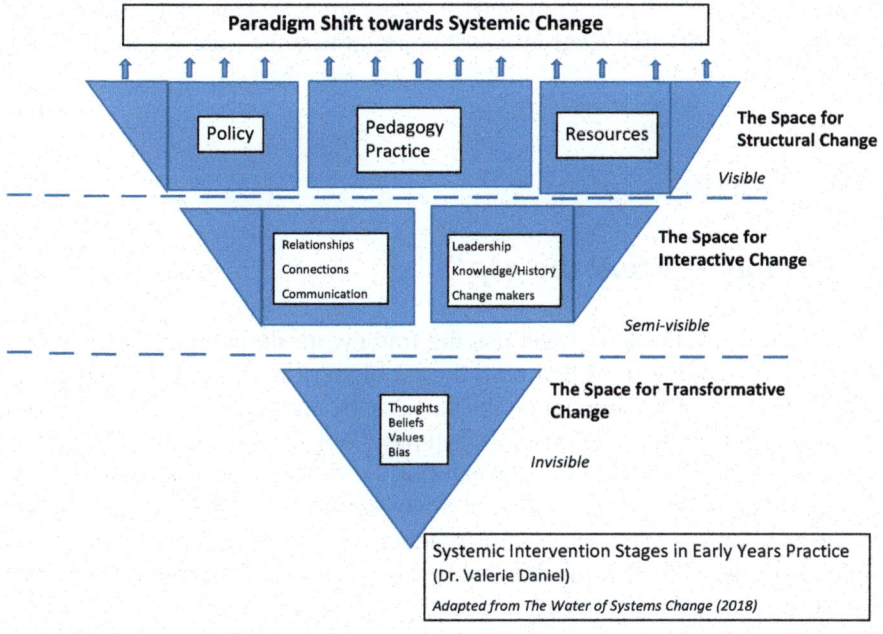

Diagram 1.1 Adapted from "The Water of Systems Change."

created a strategic plan, or declared their role but they exemplify change-making in action. Some people do not have to study and understand masses of complex theories to be changemakers; for some people, it appears to be naturally embedded in their DNA and in their actions. However, *everyone* has the capacity for changemaking; it really is just about whether that capacity is unlocked and activated within us.

It is important not to forget the *hidden* aspects of attitudes and assumptions that influence decision-making and practice within our institutions. How these conditions are identified and addressed will significantly hinder or allow for the implementation of anti-racist practice within our settings. Anti-racist practice entails social change which, in all honesty is difficult because it means challenging well-established systems in our society. The essence of this challenge is captured in the concept of "The Water of

Systems Change" (Kania et al., 2018) (Diagram 1.1). This diagram helps to categorise factors that feed into sustaining anti-racist practice in the early years.

The journey

Execution – "Mind the gap"

Throughout this book, we will use the framework depicted in Diagram 1.1 to explore the conditions that hold the problem of systemic racism in place, how these conditions impact on the early years, and how they can be shifted to embed anti-racist practice in our settings. Look out for the elements of this framework in other diagrams throughout the book. "The Water of Systems Change" provides a philosophical framework to develop an exemplary model for anti-racist policies and practices in the early years; it suggests that the odds for successful change are vastly increased by focusing on what is invisible to many, while also turning the lens on ourselves. Essentially, we won't be able to change our early years practice without fundamentally changing ourselves. The main aim is to promote equity while shifting the conditions that hold a problem in place. Change is far more sustainable when the problem is addressed on three levels: the invisible, the semi-visible, and the visible. The framework is applicable to anti-racist practice in general but the main focus for this book is the black child.

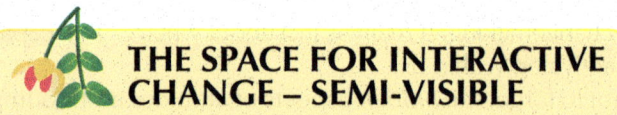

THE SPACE FOR INTERACTIVE CHANGE – SEMI-VISIBLE

Questions for reflection:

1. How is racism addressed in our early years settings?
2. What would anti-racist practice look and feel like under the headings within the space for interactive change in Diagram 1.1?

THE SPACE FOR TRANSFORMATIVE CHANGE – INVISIBLE

Question for reflection:

1. Why are the invisible factors of thoughts, beliefs, values, and bias important for our practice in the early years?

I have always been fascinated by what it takes to really effect change; more often than not, people are focused on the explicit, but I have to agree with Kania et al. (2018) that addressing the least explicit is most likely to create the most powerful conditions for sustainable change. In Jamaica we say "yu can shake a man han but yu can't shake him heart," meaning that what is in a person's mind is invisible to you despite what that person may say or do. As practitioners we have all become used to "surviving" the equalities mine-field, navigating the political correctness pathway and pole-vaulting the bar of identity politics within the work environment. After all, no one wants to lose their job and carry the stigma of being called a racist or a "woke" Black Lives Matter radical in their professional life. We have all learned to conform to the countless associated policies within our settings that must be legally adhered to, without question and usually without any deep or meaningful discussions. So, everyone (on both sides of this issue) learns to nod and smile and regurgitate the equal ops mantra when necessary.

Communication – "Talking, baulking, and then talking some more"

When we operate in a system that mainly benefits the majority, we can, just like the fish who was unaware of water, become desensitised to the environment we work in and how it can affect children who are from the ethnic minority population. It is possible that our normal practice involves reinforced concepts of race that can result in stereotyping; this is due to the historical view of race which even now continues to be ill-defined. The

5

alternative is to not be afraid to be "race-conscious" (Cerdeña et al., 2020, p. 1127) in our practice; that is, to understand race as a social construct, to understand the effects of structural racism on the children and families in our settings, and to develop strategies to identify and address structural barriers in our practice.

Instead of being "race-conscious" in early years practice, we generally tend to be nervous around race and avoid anything that might cause offence to anyone. But how can we make a difference to all the children in our care if we do not take the time to understand that we are all coming from different starting points and have different perspectives on the contentious issue of race relations? One of the most powerful things we can do is to keep talking and keep asking the hard questions, such as: do we think the issue of anti-racist practice is important enough that we create safe spaces to have meaningful conversations about racism? Is it important enough that we make time to co-construct strategies for systemic change in our practice? The answers to these questions are the starting points from which we can pursue the journey towards change.

The space for change

Systemic racism requires systemic change; that is, change that affects the whole issue instead of just parts. Systemic issues are interconnected and interdependent and cannot really be understood in isolation. If the Covid-19 pandemic has taught us anything, it is that systemic issues are never simple. In the wake of the pandemic, systemic failures have been magnified and brought into sharp focus in our healthcare system, in our education system, in our criminal justice system, in our government, and in differences within labour, productivity, and allocation of resources. To create a paradigm shift towards systemic change in early years practice is essentially to create a model towards systemic change in general; such a shift can only come about if the whole issue is addressed and unpacked to identify spaces for change.

We live in a country where the majority of the population has co-existed with diverse cultural ethnicities since World War Two, when the flood of immigration fundamentally changed the ecology of Britain's population.

Conceptualising a multicultural Britain should, ideally, have been a part of the process when the call went out to the colonies to come to help rebuild the "Motherland" after the ravages of war. The understanding was that the UK jobs market was wide open, the incentive being that there was mutual benefit in these opportunities being taken up both in terms of the reconstruction of post-war Britain and for the immigrants themselves. Unfortunately, the pressing need for immediate support appeared to outweigh any long-term vision of what Britain would look like once this support was no longer needed.

However, now that we are where we are, conceptualising multiculturalism in contemporary Britain should, ideally, be a process of reflecting on Britain's colonial history and the part it plays in structural racism. Sadly, as a society, we appear to be in a state of persistent denial regarding the reality of racism and somewhat ignorant of how it truly impacts on different ethnic groups. Early years education forms part of the UK's education sector and although it is widely viewed as a "fluffy," feel-good space, protected from the harsh realities of life, the fact is that it does not exist in a bubble; it is a smaller-scale version of our "messy" wider society. Unfortunately, our lack of a significant enough understanding of the realities of multiculturalism prevents us from creating a more equitable society; inequality negatively impacts the early years sector.

The issues surrounding racism may be structural, but they also reach deep into each person's personal values and belief systems and into the ways in which we influence children's lives, consciously and/or unconsciously contributing to inequality in society. I came across an action research project (Epstein, 1993) which was structured around the theme of "too small to notice", essentially asking whether "adults regard children in the early years of schooling as too small to notice or understand either racism or the significance given to skin colour in our society?" and whether racism is "too small a problem to be noticed when there are few, or no, children from racialised groups in the school" (Epstein, 1993, p. 317). These questions were among others asked on the theme of "too small to notice" to provide context for the project. This piece of research is just shy of 30 years old, yet the issues are still as relevant today as they were in 1993. In fact, this piece of work was so "on point" that I decided to use parts of the project as a case study. Read about Alex and his nursery classmates in the following case study.

7

CASE STUDY 1: CONSTRUCTIONS OF RACISM IN EARLY CHILDHOOD

Epstein observes that her own experience of working with young children shows that "young children [are] able not only to understand, use and construct dominant ideologies, but also to decentre and take part in deconstruction of these same ideologies … they are aware of difference and, indeed, of racism." In her research, she used a photo pack (Development Education Centre, 1986) which represented people of different nationalities in non-stereotypical roles; as an activity, children were asked to choose photos they liked or disliked and give reasons why. Epstein explained that although the word was not used, this activity quickly turned into a discussion about "racism."

"In one nursery, for example, the reaction of one child became the source of considerable discussion by the children." A child named Alex had commented negatively on a photograph depicting some black children "he described as 'blackie,' saying, 'I don't like them blackie ones.' This led to considerable confusion, since several of the white children in the class perceived Alex, himself, as 'blackie,' while he denied that he fitted this description." Alex became very distressed, which led to his classmates making comments such as "We do like blackies. I'm your friend," and "if you're nice, it's OK" in an effort to make him feel better. "One group of white children also spent some time talking about how they would not like to be called 'blackie' and speculating on how it must feel to be called, as they put it, 'bad' names" (Epstein, 1993, p. 326).

Epstein also shared that many authors have established that young children are very conscious of skin colour and often display racist feelings and express racist opinions. She further states that "it is clear that expressions of racism are hurtful to young children" and also that "it is common place that young African-Caribbean and South Asian children have been known to try to scrub their skins 'white,' but it can also be deduced from other evidence, such as Alex's distress at the suggestion that he might be 'black.'"

Epstein cautions that assuming that children are so innocent that they can't be racist actually "reinforces the status quo" and "fosters racist forms of education." She also argues that it is important to encourage children to notice and discuss racism because "if children's expressions of racism (even where they are not fully understood by the children themselves) are left uncountered and unchallenged, then the very act of refraining from challenge in itself legitimates and helps to construct racist discourses" (Epstein 1993, p. 328).

CASE STUDY EXERCISE

- Using the Epstein study (1993) alongside Kania et al.'s (2018) "The Water of Systems Change," identify themes regarding race and anti-racist practice linked to the six areas identified in Diagram 1.1.
- Discuss the relevance of practitioners "refraining from challenge" and how this may legitimate and help to construct racist discourses.
- Highlight and discuss the lessons learned to inform good anti-racist practice in the early years.

The thing about racism is that it is not just about a preference for your own kind; it is the acceptance of widespread inequality for *black and ethnic minority people* (black and ethnic minority is not terminology that I am comfortable with but in the absence of a preferable descriptive terminology that I am comfortable with, it will have to suffice for this book) across the world. This is historical and has been nurtured over time through the stereotypes that have been created around skin tones. Sadly, this has been happening for so long that it has formed a pattern of social acceptance that is hard to get rid of – a bit like a bad habit.

On a personal level, if I have a 20-a-day smoking habit, this becomes a natural aspect of my day-to-day life. To change this situation, I need to accept that this is not a good habit for my health and for the health of my family and the people around me. Even accepting this may not be enough to make the necessary changes; changing this situation will require developing and sustaining a strong desire to stop, paying attention to a habit that is normal for me and satisfies me, and then actively working against it to preserve my health and the health of all the people with whom I interact. This is, of course, easier said than done, but it *can* be done – as anyone who has ever beaten a smoking habit can tell us.

The wrong stitch

Racism on a systemic level is a whole other ball game! The way I can best describe it is like a large, elaborate heirloom tapestry that has been completed with a wrong stitch that would just require too much effort to unpick and make right. After all, the majority of the family, throughout the ages, have been quite happy displaying this tapestry and have never looked closely enough to be bothered about the wrong stitch; and, for the workers or guests who visit the family home who have noticed and are irritated by it, well, they will just have to accept it because it is too late to change it. This tapestry has been passed down from generation to generation and has been quite valuable to the owners. Over the years, a few of the owners have noticed the wrong stitch and they have spent a bit of time exploring whether this tapestry will be devalued if it is unravelled. It feels a bit like betrayal to unravel the time, effort, and work that has been put into the design of this tapestry by the family's ancestors. Over time, it has just become easier to basically "forget" about the "wrong stitch," especially as most of the family are quite happy with it. The tapestry has been framed and reframed during more recent times to draw attention away from the wrong stitch, but the stitch is becoming more noticeable as the tapestry ages and fades around it.

Whew! That was a whole thought process! I hope it makes sense to you. Now that I think about it, maybe where we are going wrong is in trying to persuade the descendants of the original designers and weavers of this tapestry to unpick and make the tapestry perfect; instead, we should convene a meeting with a new set of designers and weavers who are rich in their knowledge of the diversity of culture and complexion – the full range – and then create a new tapestry that we can all enjoy. This new tapestry would equally reflect and value our imperfections as human beings and allow us to not remain so focused on the imperfection of a piece of artwork that was, anyway, never intended for the enjoyment of all.

As a Christian, I wholly embrace the imperfection of human beings, but I equally value the concept of finding beauty in the broken. The Japanese have a deep cultural acceptance and appreciation of imperfection and of finding beauty in the broken. The wabi-sabi philosophy is about appreciating the distorted and the irregular, repairing and highlighting damage so we can all celebrate the passage of time; we are broken people in a broken world, but we can find beauty in our imperfections if we allow ourselves to do that. Slavery happened; we can't edit it out of history or repair the cracks as if it were never there. Instead, we can use humanity as the gold filler to highlight our broken history so that we can celebrate our reassembled connection as human beings and begin to value the work we have put in to repair the damage over the passage of time. If we can't accomplish this, then I suggest that we all need to try to create a whole new set of weird, wonderful, and wonky vessels that still embrace the wabi-sabi principles of harmony, transparency, respect, and tranquillity (see Figure 1.1).

We know that racism has historical roots and a disturbingly persistent ability to seek out the nutrients that keep it alive and well. In all honesty, Britain has public policies and human rights legislations that aim for a fairer society, but policies and legislations can never be enough to solve social and structural issues, or we would not continue to have issues with worker's rights, children's rights, and woman's rights, for example. Despite some of these issues being ongoing and problematic, you would be hard-pressed to find direct denial that they exist – which is a point of view that is readily available in conversations on the issue of racism. This standpoint of denial effectively stops the system from being repaired. The cracks in the system are not hairline cracks; they are sizeable cracks that require major repairs or

Figure 1.1 Wabi-sabi – beauty in the broken.

a complete rebuilding because the beams have lost bearing, the walls are leaning quite badly, and the structure is dangerously unsafe and will collapse if nothing is done.

On a personal level, we may also need to factor into this discussion that many indigenous British people may subconsciously choose to avoid knowing the depth of the issues regarding racism, as it really is not a pleasant issue to focus on. Let's be honest, who wants to deal with a steady diet of unpleasantness if they have a choice to do otherwise? As with the analogy of the habitual smoker, this level of focus is really only sustainable if there is a desire to change on a personal level, nurtured by empathy and the knowledge and understanding that we may be doing some level of harm to ourselves and to others.

Racism and the brain

As early years practitioners, we are very aware of the importance of brain development for young children. I think we may also need to be aware of how racism happens in the brain. Racism does not come from just one part of the brain; it comes from many parts of the brain working together to interact with the world around us. The part of the brain called the amygdala becomes active when we see people who are different to us and if we are not equipped to understand how to appreciate each other's differences, this can lead, knowingly or unknowingly, to treating people who are different to us unfairly. The part of the brain called the prefrontal cortex is capable of cognitive reappraisal, which we can employ as a strategy to help us interact harmoniously with people who are different to us. The prefrontal cortex is a much larger area of the brain than the amygdala and it sits at the very front of the head just beneath the forehead. The prefrontal cortex is designed to calm the amygdala down, but due to any number of reasons it may not be doing a very good job of this regulation. When our prefrontal cortex is working well, it helps us to realise that just because our amygdala has recognised a difference and is making a big deal out of it, does not mean that it is accurate or that we have to heed what it is telling us. Cognitive reappraisal helps us to understand that, generally, people who are different to us are not usually a threat to us in any way (see Figure 1.2).

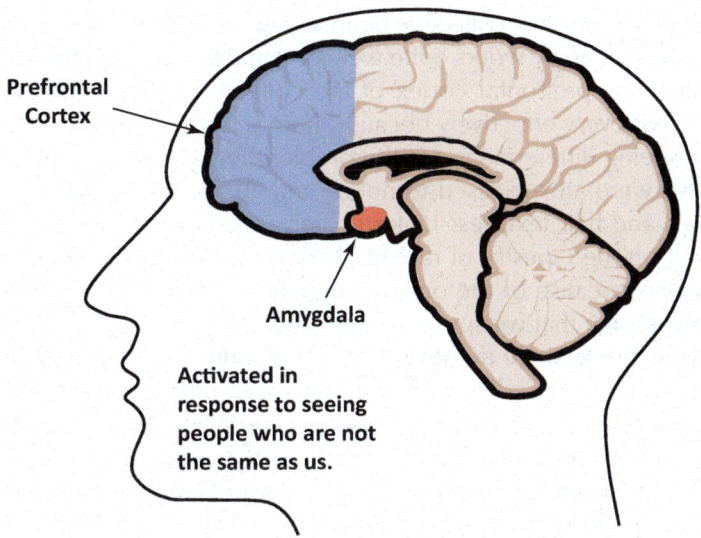

Prefrontal Cortex

Amygdala

Activated in response to seeing people who are not the same as us.

Figure 1.2 The brain response.

Sadly, this assumption of difference as a threat can be present even in the early years. Let us think about this in this way: what do we, as practitioners, do when we feel that something might be a threat in the early years? We put measures in place to control the threat and manage the potential for harm.

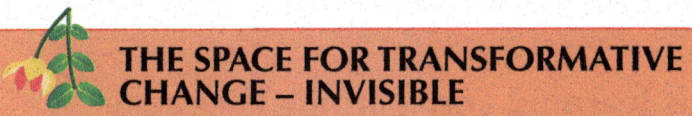

THE SPACE FOR TRANSFORMATIVE CHANGE – INVISIBLE

Questions for reflection:

1. How can we assess whether we could knowingly or unknowingly be reducing the potential of children who we see as different to us, in an effort to control them because they are stereotypically perceived as being potentially harmful?
2. How can we as leaders and practitioners in the early years put measures in place to help our prefrontal cortex do a better job?

I am going to attribute a collective brain to systemic racism to try to explain a system that seemingly works quite well for some but not for others. It would appear that the prefrontal cortex of the collective brain in social systems does not work very effectively because there is a perception of threat. In my opinion, seeing difference is not the problem; in fact, how amazing would it be if we were all socialised to notice and appreciate the wide variety of skin tones and hair textures? Unfortunately, cognitive reappraisal does not work well on the tapestry of racism; there is a reluctance to make sustainable change because of the ongoing benefits of that "wrong stitch" in the traditional design that we spoke about earlier.

As practitioners, we do not have a lot of influence to outrightly change systemic racism, but collectively we can create a measured undercurrent that ripples beneath the surface, just strong enough that it pulls others along without being hazardous. Someone is bound to say that this is a utopian viewpoint; my response would be that we are not aiming for perfection, we are aiming to develop a realistic approach which acknowledges our present human problems and to create an infrastructure that is actively working towards equality. There is no perfect society for imperfect human beings: this should lead us to accept that there is no best way to live, because variations in people's circumstances means that *our* best is not *their* best. Whilst we may never have personal, political, economic, and social perfection, structural cognitive reappraisal would go a long way in embedding fairness in social systems. Inequality has been hundreds of years in the making so we have to accept that equality will be a process over time, if and when there is a commitment to truly learn from each other.

Change is learning and learning is change

Probably the most disregarded aspect of learning is the process of *unlearning*. We have all acquired knowledge from our experiences and while most of this knowledge may be viable, some of it will most definitely be outdated. To move forward, we have to embrace the concept of continuous learning: the process of unlearning, learning, and relearning in order to evolve. It is not impossible to unlearn if, as leaders in early years practice, we foster a sense of willingness in our practice instead of demanding compliance. As early years practitioners, what do we know about learning?

Learning means:

- Processing the unfamiliar to grasp new ideas and allow them to take hold.
- Being open to a fresh viewpoint and not limiting our capacity to learn.
- Being open to explore ideas without fear or being worried about looking or feeling stupid.

The best way to understand that change is learning and learning is change, is by considering a child's capacity for learning. We know that children learn by being fully immersed in the process; their five senses are engaged, and they learn from trial and error. To change how we unlearn some of our past knowledge, we need to tap into our inner child to regenerate that sense of curiosity that makes us want to investigate, understand, and empathise with the perspectives of others.

Learning needs:

- A safe, stimulating environment with opportunities to repeat and practice what we learn.
- Active engagement, including observing, listening, exploring, asking questions, responding.
- Trust, honesty, courage, and encouragement.

Learning goals include:

- Choosing to be involved in our learning; self-empowerment to seek out learning in our own time, e.g., books to read, seeking opportunities to speak to someone different to us.
- Setting clear and challenging goals that encourage motivation and self-reliance (not too much at once!).
- Making mini successes during the process clear, so that everyone feels socially and emotionally connected to the process of change.
- Ensuring there is continuous support for changemakers and that we are checking in to help each other out.

Just like the children in our care, learning is different for different people. I don't know how you react to learning something new; I have just had an upgrade on my iPhone and my son jumped on this right away and was working with features I personally do not believe that hand-held devices should have! (This of course is an excuse for my resistance to handling the new complexity that comes with the upgrade and the frustration in recognising the need to be agile in the face of my complacency with my old phone.) Some of us may want to wait until learning feels comfortable but to be honest, real learning is rarely comfortable. Especially in the cases of unlearning and relearning, we have to be prepared to let go of the familiar and open up our minds to the unfamiliar.

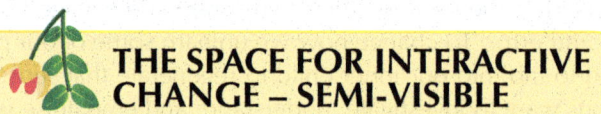

THE SPACE FOR INTERACTIVE CHANGE – SEMI-VISIBLE

Team exercise:

- What would you do today if you were not afraid?
- In your personal life.
- In your professional practice.

Anti-racist practice – "It's the obvious choice, isn't it?"

Racism has sadly been framed mainly as an issue of morality, and as such, we generally hold the opinion that racism is wrong. It is therefore widely seen as a problem perpetuated by "bad" people. We will address this in more detail later on in the book, but it is worthwhile noting that some of the nicest, kindest people have ingrained, and sometimes dormant, racist views and ideologies floating about in their mental spaces. The result of framing racism as a purely moral issue is that even when acts of unconscious racism occur, people feel accused of wrongdoing and, of course, they naturally become defensive. When we become defensive, a "fight or flight" response is triggered, and this does not create a mental space where we can be calm or rational.

Racism has become the subject of an ongoing debate about validity, often with a school of thought that promotes the idea that talking about race and the issues surrounding race is unhelpful, disruptive to the smooth running of the country, and damaging to race relations. Let's take a second to relate this idea to our practice in the early years; we know that ignoring issues that interfere with the smooth running of the day would be similar to involving children only in activities that keep them occupied, quiet, "out of our hair" so we can get on with other things, but not meaningfully engaged in their education. Having children mindlessly watching television most of the time or *only* involved in activities that keep them quiet is definitely easier from an operational perspective but we know, from the perspective of learning and development, that activities that never challenge children's thinking or create opportunities for them to learn, is not better for them. So, I suggest that we need to learn and understand the concept of race as a social construct and not as a biological fact.

It is by no means a stretch of the imagination to state that the current structures and ideologies that uphold racism take a toll not only on children and families but also on how the human race develops. As part of our assessment of anti-racist practice in our settings, we, as practitioners, should consider the racism and inequality that is experienced by parents and how it affects their parenting. The support we offer from our settings can make a difference in overcoming structural barriers and allowing children to thrive (creating that undercurrent ripple we spoke about earlier).

THE SPACE FOR STRUCTURAL CHANGE – VISIBLE

Questions for reflection:

1. What would you put in place in your setting to open up conversations with practitioners regarding race and the impact of inequality on children, staff, and parents?
2. How would you approach fostering a discrimination-free early years environment with staff, children, and parents?

The wider issues

The *Race Relations Act 1965* and the *Race Relations Act 1968* were amended by the *Race Relations Amendment Act 2000* which imposed a statutory duty on public bodies to promote racial equality and also to ensure that there were procedures in place to prevent discrimination. This Act was then repealed by the *Equality Act 2010* which consolidated previous discrimination law in the UK and clearly identified "protected characteristics," of which race is one. The *Equality Act 2010* does not, however, automatically protect those who fall under "protected characteristics" from the day-to-day injustices they face, but it is nevertheless a vital piece of legislation that is essential to the ideals of a just and equitable society. Despite this, the *Equality Act 2010* is under constant threat from the current Conservative government, which only serves to tell us how fragile the concept of equality is for black and ethnic minority children and families.

Understanding how to make changes to our current landscape of social inequality necessitates having knowledge of the function of race in society and having an even deeper understanding of how the current concept of race continually reproduces and normalises the idea of a natural social hierarchy within society. Race is not a singular entity. It is an interweaving of ideas from many disciplines in education including geography, biology, physiology, philosophy, sociology, religion, and history and, ultimately, the fusion of these ideas, which is then used to typify whole populations of people. Race is not a theory; it is a framework that builds on the persistent nurturing of the idea of inherent racial differences based on biological factors and genetic coding linked to intelligence, character, physical abilities, and personality traits. We know that research has debunked these myths so, as early childhood practitioners, how can we navigate anti-racist practice despite the persistence of these flawed ideologies? My answer to this question is that we become informed and that we work the steps.

False narratives surrounding race

In recent times there has been quite a bit of uproar regarding critical race theory (CRT), an academic concept that explores race as a social construct and racism not just as the product of individual bias but also as an ideology that is embedded in public policies and legal systems. CRT is not a curriculum that is taught in the classroom; it is a theory that helps changemakers to focus on outcomes for children and families who experience racism rather than just continually mulling about the beliefs of individuals. The public outcry against CRT stems from the belief that CRT presents all white people as racist; but what the theory actually states is that racism is an aspect of everyday life and everybody (white, black, ethnic minority) can, with no intention of being racist, nevertheless make, and act on, decisions that fuel racism. Boakye (2022) tells us that as a black man and an English teacher, the concept of "whiteness" is a default: "that's what makes it so pervasive. It's where whiteness is seen as normal to the extent that challenging it would be akin to insanity, like if I started running around screaming at everyone to consider why the sky is blue" (p. 9). Promoting false narratives around strategies that support anti-racist practice is a primal response by some powerful and influential people to continue to protect the concept of "whiteness" as a default and these strategies continue to confuse changemakers and derail any action to create a more equitable society.

The Commission on Race and Ethnic Disparities (CRED) was established in 2020 to look at race and ethnic disparities in the UK in the wake of Black Lives Matter protests following the murder of George Floyd. It found that while the UK does not yet enjoy racial equality, it is not a country that operates on institutionally racist policies and systems. Whether I agree or disagree with this sentiment is of little consequence, because, as practitioners, we have to work with what we have. The section of the report that addresses "What we think about race" states: "Racism is both real and socially constructed. Society has 'defined racism down' to encompass attitudes and behaviours that would not have been considered racist in the past" (Commission on Race and Ethnic Disparities, 2021). I am not entirely sure whose perspective was being reported on in this statement and I am not entirely sure how we define racism "up" or "down," but as early years professionals we need a clear definition of racism and how it currently impacts the children in our care. Jones (2000) advises us that institutional racism is revealed in a number of ways but also presents as:

- Inaction in the face of need
- Differential access to quality education, sound housing, gainful employment, appropriate medical facilities, and a clean environment.

(p. 1212)

If as practitioners we come across issues of inequality on a daily basis, then I think it is fair to assume that despite racism not being as overt as in the past, it is nevertheless embedded in the culture, in systems, and in the law; and is oftentimes manifested as inherited disadvantage within black and ethnic minority communities. No matter how we approach this issue of anti-racist practice in the early years, we cannot escape racism as complex and multi-factorial. Jones (2000) designed a theoretical framework to explore racism on three levels, which helps us all to understand a little bit more about how we find ourselves operating in ways that may advantage some children and not others. I have taken the liberty of creating a diagram from Jones' framework (Diagram 1.2).

Diagram 1.2 highlights institutional/systemic racism as generated from the historical legacy of racism and also as structural within social systems. The aspect of personally mediated racism and internalised racism, indicates how structural racism is experienced in society. Research tells us that the intergenerational social disadvantage that often accompanies early childhood inequality is perpetuated by systemic racism. However, examining racial disparities as a factor of social disadvantage appears to be routinely avoided, or excused away as being any number of other community issues. We know that poor outcomes for young children are driven by socioeconomic factors, but for black communities, social and racial issues are not mutually exclusive. So, trying to address social issues as separate from racial issues, as suggested by the CRED Report (2021), will only continue to leave a massive gap in our ability to make real change towards anti-racist practice in the early years. As practitioners, we probably find it quite easy to see how inequality victimises the children who experience it; it may be a bit more difficult to truly unpick how inequality victimises those who benefit from it. Think of it like this: in a family with two children, one child is treated well and given everything they need and more, to the point, sometimes, of being overindulged; the other child is merely tolerated and grudgingly given just enough to survive and is generally not treated very well. How are these two children harmed by their parents?

Surely we all have certain family traditions that seem normal to us but which might, unbeknownst to us, appear strange to others? In fact, the only time we realise that some of our habits might be seen as a little weird to others is when we are away from home and we behave in ways that are natural to us until someone says "Why are you doing that?" If what someone else considers to be weird does not harm anyone, then I think we have to learn

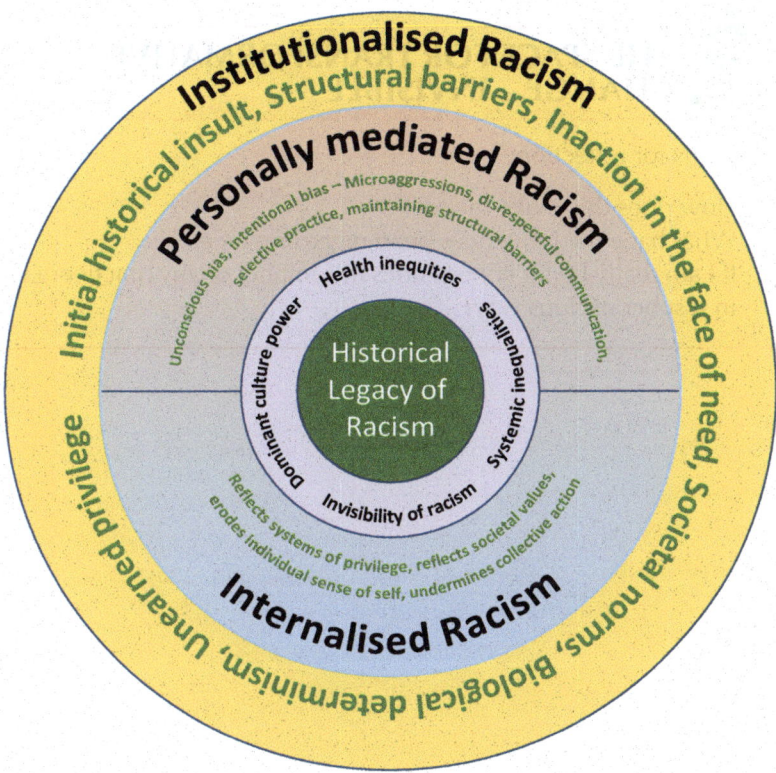

Diagram 1.2 A theoretical framework for understanding levels of racism in UK society adapted from Jones (2000).

to live and let live; but if our habit constitutes harm for others in any way, then we may need to put a little more effort into noticing how we behave and how it may affect other people negatively even when that is not the intention. This is a call for all of us to refresh our minds and our hearts. For anyone who finds themselves sadly and hopelessly addicted to TikTok, you know there is a filter for everything! My proposition is that we purposefully view the issue of racism through the filters of love, respect, and human dignity. Furthermore, I suggest that change for a more equitable society can only truly be actualised with the essential and invaluable tools of *true* self-reflection and self-inquiry.

THE SPACE FOR TRANSFORMATIVE CHANGE – INVISIBLE

Questions for reflection:

1. How does this make me feel?
2. What have my influences been regarding race?
3. If I am really being honest, does this impact on my practice? Even in a subconscious way?

A short history of racism

"Mum, what do you hope to gain from this chapter?"

My son asked me what I was hoping to gain from this chapter, and I had to think long and hard about what I wanted to achieve beyond regurgitating facts that hammer home the point that racism exists. I had to give some real thought to what I want my readers to gain from these facts. After deep consideration, I decided that I have three aims:

- To create a sense of understanding about how we got to a place where we unconsciously or consciously treat people differently based on perceptions of race.
- To understand the impact we have on others.
- To see racism through the gaze of marginalised communities and to be able to create a sense of empathy for fellow human beings on both sides of this issue.

To set the stage I decided to create a diagram that depicts racism in contemporary Britain using a stoplight system (Diagram 2.1).

Racism is not manifested, experienced, or executed in a consistent manner; on any given day, anyone can hold multiple perspectives on race depending on time, place, and circumstance. Essentially, people are people; there are some people who hold a mantra of hate far more strongly than others, for various reasons, and this phenomenon is apparent in all races. However, because the history of racial discrimination that is categorised as "white" and "non-white" is generally told through the gaze of colonialism, it would seem rational to believe that racism may exist in a blind spot for many white people. Even if there is some level of awareness, it is feasible

DOI: 10.4324/9781003247807-2

Full stop. Not affected and therefore not consciously aware of the impact of racism.

Stationary. Denial of racism – unable to see racism in ourselves but may possibly be able to pick out blatantly racist behaviours of others.

Colour blind – It is hard to change something you cannot see.

Mainstream culture – assumption of consensus, you chose to be here so this is how we are, 'like it or lump it', there is no need for change.

Space of inertia

STOP

Inequity is invisible

'**Good things happen to good people bad things happen to bad people' – 'Just Society' concept.**

Conditioned to believe and accept that some people are of less value and people of other races infringe on 'our' way of life and 'our' values – **symbolic threat, hidden in the fabric of society.**

Covert racism – microaggression, gaslighting, rationalization, unconscious bias – **subtle and pervasive.**

Keep your head down – don't make waves, things will settle down, stop talking about it and life will go back to normal. Not motivated to change or else feeling powerless to change – **passivism, apathy towards systems of racial disadvantage.**

Parallel culture – victims of racism reduce social and cultural contact with the majority population in response to recognizing that they are unwanted. Majority population expects marginalized communities to know their place.

Space of apathy

WAIT

Inequity is semi-visible

Defensive behavior. Openly dismiss victims of racism as over-sensitive, ungrateful complainers, liars, people who play the race card. Defend acts of unintentional racism.

Hostile reaction to people who speak about their experiences of racial discrimination.

Jaded justifications as to why racist behaviours are justified **Accusations of reverse racism/anti-white racism** – I'm not the racist, **YOU** are the racist! You are racist against white people!

Overt racism – a conscious choice of racist beliefs, attitudes, actions – protect what we have at all costs – even **violence. Ready to be comfortable with being uncomfortable – allies.** Ready to embrace the awkward and painful process of change – **activism – protests, rioting, violent response to a perceived threat to the way of life as it should be – motivated to actively work to maintain racist ideologies.**

Counterculture – Diametrically opposed to the values and norms of society. **Ready for action – motivated for positive change; to actively work to dismantle racist ideologies.**

Space of activity

MOVE

Inequity is visible

Diagram 2.1 A snapshot of racism in contemporary Britain.

to believe that white British people, in general, might be conditioned into thinking that this is the way things are supposed to be, without being aware that this is a conscious thought.

Diagram 2.1 attempts to depict the multidimensional state of racism as it exists in contemporary Britain. The diagram can help to pinpoint where we are on the journey to a more equitable society but it is also my hope that knowledge, understanding, and empathy will shift us all into "the green space"; the space of activity, at the point where we are ready for positive change. As "normal" human beings, we are generally hardwired to shun pain and veer away from anything that makes us uncomfortable, so I strongly believe that if we do not activate motivation during this journey, then we will quickly return to a place that feels comfortable and familiar and park there, in the spaces of inertia or apathy. Let's be honest; it is exhausting to do the right thing most of the time! It takes passion and motivation to implement change. Look at it this way: if we are plugged into our own personal playlist all the time and we never take our earphones out to listen to the music of others, then the chances are that we will never know, experience, or care about the beauty of different kinds of music. How sad is that? I love that I can't resist my natural response to dance expressively in appreciation to reggae music or to line dance to country music or become totally lost in listening to jazz or classical music. Music feeds my soul and I want to experience it all. I might not like it all, but I can appreciate it all.

A brief historical timeline of the evolution of systemic racism

"Those who cannot remember the past are condemned to repeat it."
– George Santayana (1905)

The history of racism is not the same as the history of slavery, even though they do overlap. The history of racism extends way beyond slavery in terms of time and form and includes explicit forms of harm, that is, conscious speech, action, or behaviour that openly demonstrates racist attitudes and beliefs; for example, slavery, segregation, xenophobia, genocide, white-supremacist ideology, hate crimes. The history of racism also includes continuous implicit harm, that is, giving "plausible deniability" to those who subvert, restrict, distort, and gaslight the victims of racism; for example, stereotyping, racial inequalities, microaggression, right through to structural/systemic racism, that is, policies and systems that harm the health and livelihood of the victims of racism; for example, job seeking, disproportionate and unfair criminal justice and law enforcement systems, inequity in housing, healthcare, and medical systems. That being said, it has become really clear that this chapter will mainly be linked to the "space for transformative change" – a space that speaks to our thoughts, beliefs, values, and personal bias; and also the "space for interactive change" – how we look at relationships, connections, communication, how knowledge and history changed the course of people's lives, and how leadership and changemakers can produce change in our current circumstances.

The 15th century – the discovery of new worlds

Those of us who work in the early years are very familiar with the "in-group"–"out-group" mentality. We see it in action every day when children exercise their friendship preferences and their ability to manipulate who plays with whom. This concept is especially problematic when our brains use automatic systems to categorise people into "people who are like me" and "people who are different to me". If we view racism through the lens of team sports, we have a better understanding of the "in-group"–"out-group" dynamic. Obviously, we are going to cheer for our team because they are in our "in-group" category (Diagram 2.2).

This mentality has probably been present since the dawn of time when people operated on a more tribalistic level, but the history of racism as we know it today is indeed a Western European phenomenon which has roots traceable back to the 15th century and Christopher Columbus and the "doctrine of discovery of new worlds". I imagine, on a purely humanistic level, that this venture was conducted in the spirit of human progress and with no intention of changing the course of cultural history of whole populations of people. However, when other people were encountered during these travels, interaction with them was shaped through the lens of white Western Christianity. Europeans were greeted with unfamiliar people with totally different ways of life and, as we understand it, Europeans at that time perceived themselves to be the personification of progressive humanity. This is not an unusual way of

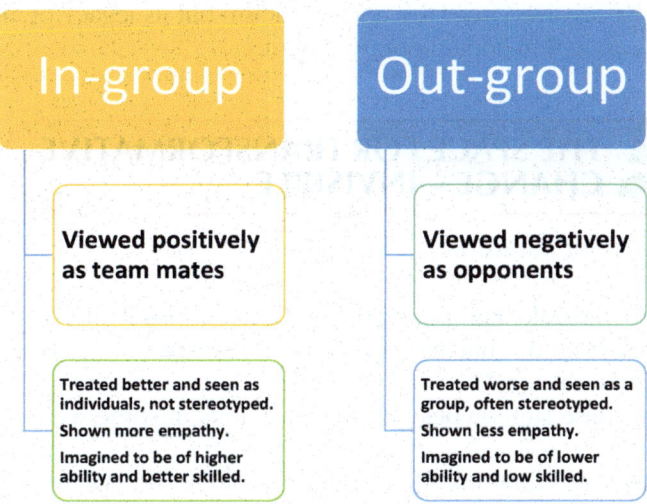

Diagram 2.2 The "in-group"–"out-group" mentality.

thinking, as research shows that people have a natural tendency to "illusionary superiority" (Van Yprern & Buunk, 1991) or what is more simply known as "superiority bias". The doctrine of "discovery" carries the justification of doing "God's work", which initiated a colonial mentality that was strengthened by the self-proclaimed superiority of the "discoverers" and their perceived inferiority of the "discovered". I imagine that the "discoverers" would have absolutely believed that they were doing good, at least initially.

Alongside the ability to navigate the seas, in the 1400s Europeans also invented the printing press and capitalised on this to widely disseminate images that would become stereotypes of the "savages" they had "discovered". This helped to rapidly spread the ideology of race and white supremacy at this point in history. The issue of a racial hierarchy became nuanced when different races were phased into the manufactured racial classification, but it was always with the knowledge that everyone else was inferior to people from Western Europe. A combination of a pseudo-scientific, biblical, and theological justification reinforced this specific kind of white supremacist racism, which became a global phenomenon. The kind of racism that has since evolved and developed from this phenomenon has deeply shaped mindsets and human interactions all around the world. The current context of racism has evolved from this ancient racism but its legacy of inequality is still deeply rooted in contemporary racism.

THE SPACE FOR TRANSFORMATIVE CHANGE – INVISIBLE

Questions for reflection:

1. What would Europeans have observed about the people they "discovered" that led them to label them as "backward" and "sinful savages"?
2. Do these stereotypes exist in our minds in some way in current times?
3. What do you think Africa was like before the slave trade?
4. How can the evolution of racism affect us in our practice in the early years?

The 16th and 17th centuries – the era of Britain's dominance in the slave trade

At the start of the 16th century, Britain's interest in the continent of Africa was mainly about African produce such as ivory, gold, indigo, and pepper. Britain became involved in the slave trade in the 1600s and was dominant in it between 1640 and 1807, when the British slave trade was officially abolished. The National Archives explain that from 1660 "the British Crown passed various acts and granted charters to enable companies to settle, administer and exploit British interests on the West Coast of Africa and to supply slaves to the American colonies." During the time that Britain was actively involved in the slave trade, it is estimated that they transported 3.1 million Africans to the Caribbean, North and South America, and to other countries. Only 2.7 million Africans survived the inhumane conditions under which they were transported. Let that sink in! Four hundred thousand people died! Let me put 400,000 deaths into perspective. As of May 2022, at the time of writing, 177,000 people have died from Covid-19. Think about how these deaths have affected us all in various ways. These 400,000 slaves had families, communities they belonged to, hopes, dreams, and aspirations. This was conceivably the beginning of publicly erasing the truth of black humanity for reasons best known to the Europeans at this point in history.

It is obvious that racism outdates slavery, but racism made it a lot easier to deem slavery to be justifiable and perfectly reasonable at this time. This was a period of gross atrocities perpetrated against black people. Rape, branding, mutilation, beating, black men being forced to procreate with their mothers, sisters, and daughters to ensure a steady stock of slaves, punishments at the whim of white masters, the sale of children and forced separation of families: these are among the methods used to violate and degrade black people. The graphicness of some of the atrocities is triggering for me and would only serve to divert the course of this book, so, as I am sure my readers have the general gist, we will avoid any more of the gory details. I do find it interesting, however, that the cruelty committed against black people resulted in black people being labelled as savages. British plantation records show that slaves were dehumanised and reduced to being property: itemized in inventories, recorded for tax reasons, and detailed in wills as transferable goods. This practice is more succinctly known as chattel slavery. Chattel slavery allowed human beings to be considered as personal possessions and to be casually ascribed a value in sterling as a sale price.

The stereotyping and dehumanisation of black people still continues, 400 plus years later, only in more sophisticated forms. We only need to look to daily news reports and a significant world event such as the murder of George Floyd to confirm that a white policeman kneeling across the neck of a black man for nine minutes and twenty-nine seconds and casually depriving him of oxygen to the point of killing him, in full view of the public, means that this black man was not considered to be quite human. All this, just because it was suspected that Floyd had paid with a counterfeit $20 bill in a store. This single event caused me to stop sleepwalking through my life and to accept that I needed to be the change if I wanted change to happen.

Britain has been quite successful in airbrushing its slave-owning and slave-trading past; retouching and editing out the blemishes and imperfections. Distancing from the unpleasantness of Britain's gruesome past was quite easily done as the main event of slavery happened 3,000 miles away in the Caribbean and, technically, slavery has never had a legal basis in Britain. The disappearance of huge parts of British history is most definitely a contributing factor to British people not understanding how they uphold white supremacy. I deeply acknowledge that the average white person may have no racist intent at all; indeed, because they have consistently received a watered-down version of facts, they might be shocked to discover the truth about British history and how the injustices of the past are destined to be repeated.

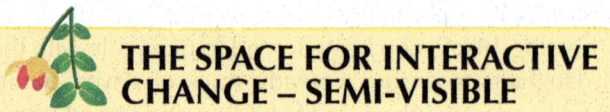

THE SPACE FOR INTERACTIVE CHANGE – SEMI-VISIBLE

Questions for reflection:

1 Highlight and discuss any historical facts which may seem surprising.
2. How do you think colonial rule has impacted on education and how is early years education affected by these legacies?

The 17th and 18th centuries – the Age of Enlightenment

Fast forward to the 17th and 18th centuries, when the impact of Europe's global influences intensified during the Age of Enlightenment, an intellectual and philosophical movement that used reason, scientific method, and the concept of progress to create "better societies" and "better people" based on a Western European classification of humanity. This, of course, is now recognised to have been a very narrow field of so-called objectivity, which allowed for the ranking of humanity in terms of racial hierarchy, with white Europeans at the top and black Africans at the bottom. These pseudo-scientific theories have been vehemently exposed as false but, in many ways, continue to be central to contemporary society.

The stories of how, during the 17th and 18th centuries, numerous British families became exorbitantly wealthy from trading slaves, and from the sale of slave-produced products, are usually told in a way that romanticises the British Empire. In my mind, I can only compare it to the mass dumping of the bodies of slaves into deep graves and then the surrounding area being landscaped with the most gorgeous, fragrant rose gardens. White British people generally tend to see only the beauty of the garden and only smell the fragrance of the roses, while non-white British people generally tend to cry about the bodies of their ancestors which have been used to fertilise the soil that allows these beautiful flowers to grow and thrive; they only smell the stench of death that seeps up through the earth, drowning out the fragrance of the roses. A powerful contrast in perspectives on the same experience, this is essentially the experience of racism for most white and non-white British people: the seen versus the unseen.

George Orwell compared Britain to a wealthy family that is committed to maintaining a guilty silence about the source of its wealth. Despite the secrecy, the rewards of the transatlantic slave trade were plain to see at the time: the prosperous slave ports, the grand homes, the thriving industrial cities with jobs created to boost the economy, and the coffee and tobacco shops that were opening up in British cities. The slave trade also generated enormous wealth for traders, plantation owners, and financial investors. During this time, parliament passed over one hundred acts to support and protect the slave trade; Britain was undeniably wealthier because of it and British citizens were becoming used to enjoying the benefits of the slave-produced commodities that had vastly enhanced their way of life.

THE SPACE FOR TRANSFORMATIVE CHANGE – INVISIBLE

Questions for reflection:

1. How can even a subconscious belief in the pseudo-scientific classification of black people as being on the bottom of a made-up racial hierarchy affect how we deal with black and ethnic minority children in our day-to-day practice?

The 18th and 19th centuries – the era of the abolition movement

In the late 18th century and during the 19th century, England had a population of around 1,500 black people, mainly found in the major port cities of

London, Bristol, and Liverpool but also in market towns and villages. Most worked in low-paid or unpaid domestic service, even though it was established that slavery had no legal basis in England. It appears that the law was interpreted ambiguously by slave-owners who continued to treat most of the slaves they owned as their property even after they had returned to live in England. During this time there was a movement calling for the end of the slave trade and, later, for an end to slavery itself. The abolition movement was widely attributed to William Wilberforce, but also included a collective effort of grass-roots organisation, black resistance, international interest, and strong leadership. The actions and influence of changemakers to effect positive change during this time of turbulence is a powerful message for us all.

Abolitionism is arguably the most successful countercultural reform movement of the 18th and 19th centuries. Legislation to end Britain's involvement in the slave trade was finally passed in both the House of Commons and the House of Lords; the bill received royal assent in March 1807 and the trade was made illegal from May 1, 1807. It did, however, take 20 more years before Britain's involvement in the slave trade ended and 26 years before British colonial slavery ended in the Caribbean, in 1833. Sometimes it is easy to forget the reality of the experience and how every stage of the movement was a bitter struggle of anti-slavery activists being pitted against pro-slavery interests. The abolition movement lost momentum for a while after the 1792 September Massacres, sometimes referred to as the "First Terror" of the French Revolution.

You might understandably ask what the French Revolution had to do with the abolition of slavery in Britain. The simple answer is that the September Massacres were widely publicised as proof of the horrors of countercultural movements and of any form of activism for equality. This had some success in frightening off supporters of the abolition movement. Interestingly, pro-slavery advocates labelled abolitionists "unpatriotic Jacobin sympathisers bent on the subversion of the British Constitution" (Oldfield, 2021). Now why does this seem familiar? Oh yes! "Woke, left-wing sympathisers bent on the subversion of the British Constitution" is the loud and acrimonious backlash used to attempt to cancel any efforts to combat inequality in contemporary society. The strategy is at least 300 years old and still working to subvert equality! Imagine being deemed unpatriotic for not wanting to enslave other human beings!

We need to understand that the slave trade and the plantation system of slavery underpinned Britain's imperialistic expansion, greased the wheels of British industry, and created significant links between the economy and state power. The slave trade was considered an essential and necessary part of the British Empire even though Britain was the largest Christian empire and slavery, and the slave trade, would surely have been counterintuitive in terms of Christian dogma. The moral ambiguity of the British Empire meant that for almost 150 years, Britain was the dominant force behind transporting millions of enslaved African men, women, and children, subjecting them to forced labour, denying them basic rights, leading to the solidification of racist ideals and the persistence of a pseudoscience that continues to be used to justify the treatment of black people as subhuman.

Despite Christianity, a number of factors had to come into play to steer the abolitionist movement into reality; increasing slave revolts in the colonies challenged the continued viability of slavery; the ownership of large parts of India was generating huge profit for the British Empire; the Reform Bill of 1832 increased the size of the British electorate and created 67 new constituencies, which was an opportunity for abolitionists to put pressure on their parliamentary candidates. The economic decline of slavery was also a contributing factor as there was an oversupply of slave-produced commodities such as sugar, and British merchants were struggling to re-export. There were also far more profitable uses for ships than for the slave trade. Despite the drive towards the Emancipation Act of 1833, anti-slavery activists had to concede twenty million pounds' worth of compensation for the loss of "property" to be granted to slave-owners. It is worth noting that no reparations have been paid to those who were emancipated from a grossly inhumane forced labour system that only benefited the British Empire.

The 800,000-plus people who were eventually emancipated were left to fend for themselves in a system that was stacked against them because of lingering racism. The constitutional system that pressed for civil and political rights for the emancipated chose instead to treat the emancipated slaves as dependents rather than citizens – another blow to the full independence of people of African descent. At this point, Britain introduced an "apprenticeship" system that was an integral part of the Emancipation Act. After 1833, Indian and Chinese labourers were transported to the Caribbean to work on the plantations, apparently in response to the labour shortage from slave emancipation. Work conditions were harsh, with long hours and low wages and fueled by the narrative of an "hierarchisation of oppression" which is ultimately about the supremacy of whiteness and the power to arrange, classify, and dispense this hierarchy.

> Practically, an immigrant is in the hands of the employer to whom he is bound. He cannot leave him; he cannot live without work; he can only get such work and on such terms as the employer chooses to set him; and all those necessities are enforced, not only by the inevitable influence of his isolated and dependent position, but by the terrors of imprisonment and the prospect of losing both labour and wages.
>
> (Beaumont, 1871)

> No fair-minded man will, I think, hesitate to say the system is a monstrous system, iniquitous in itself, based on fraud and maintained by force.
>
> (Gokhale, 1912)

The two accounts above powerfully inform how racist ideologies were used to inform more imaginative ways of using non-white people in forced labour to maintain the wealth of the British Empire. Kempadoo (2017), expands on the context of a colour-blind concept of race in regard to the indentured workers who came to live and work in the Caribbean. She explains that

> the Caribbean indentureship experience however, was 'colour-blind'—notions of race were not foundational to the system, even while constructs of racial difference saturated indentureship and were used to justify the harsh treatment of some workers, and at times the privileging of others.
>
> (Kempadoo, 2017, p. 60)

If we were ever in any doubt of the legacy of slavery and its impact on the modern and dubious concept of "colour-blind" racism, which in the 18th and 19th centuries allowed for "the harsh treatment of some workers" while "privileging" others, we only need to look at how racism is manifested in prejudice between different ethnic minority populations and their stratified interactions with the white majority in contemporary Britain.

We often hear how mass immigration from the West Indies changed the socio-cultural landscape of Britain, but I am unable to find any real references to how Britain changed the socio-cultural landscape of Africa, the Caribbean, or the Americas. We need to remember that mass immigration to Britain was invited and also spare a thought for how disruptive British intervention must have been to the way of life of people, in whatever part of the world they lived, bearing in mind that dehumanisation has never been a part of the white historical experience. It is interesting to note that a third of the British population still believe that British colonies were better off for being a part of the British Empire (Guardian, 2020). It would be interesting to hear which bits are perceived as "better" for the people of the Caribbean, and if the underlying context is still primarily nostalgic for the past when people from the colonies "knew their place".

The first half of the 20th century – the era of the world wars

West Indians and Africans first came to Britain as much needed manpower to fight in the First World War. Sixteen thousand soldiers were recruited and 4,500 volunteers came forward but the racism they faced was extreme; they were portrayed as demons or apes, given poor accommodation and unsuitable clothing for the winter, and 19 West Indian soldiers died in Seaford training camp. West Indian soldiers were subjected to indignities such as having to clean toilets for white soldiers and white soldiers were given pay rises whilst the West Indians were not. They were rightfully upset but when they retaliated, it resulted in 60 West Indian soldiers being tried and convicted of mutiny.

During the Second World War 16,000 West Indians volunteered to fight alongside British soldiers. Approximately 6,000 of them served with the Royal Air Force and the Royal Canadian Air Force. This is relevant for me on a personal level as my father served in the Royal Air Force. I know for a fact that he was only 15 years old at the time and I have first-hand accounts of how he was subjected to racism. During this research it surprised me to discover that other volunteers from Jamaica were also just 15 years old and, like my dad, they really had no idea of the level of danger associated with this volunteer mission. There were approximately 110 women who were deployed between the Women's Auxiliary Air Force and the Auxiliary Territorial Service, and 1,000 volunteers formed the Caribbean Regiment for the Army Service and were deployed overseas to the Middle East and Italy in 1944.

Once again, West Indian soldiers felt that because they were British, being in Britain would feel like "home away from home" but instead they were faced with struggling to adapt to the cold climate and once again faced with dealing with rampant racism as a remaining legacy of slavery. West Indian service men were given the opportunity to return home after the war with a sum of money as an incentive (I also know this as a fact because my dad took his money and returned to Jamaica) or they were given the option to remain in Britain, which many chose to do, essentially solidifying multiculturalism. West Indians who married local women caused uproar among members of the public who were outraged about mixed-race relationships.

The second half of the 20th century – the Age of Austerity and the Windrush generation

The Second World War ended in September 1945 and Britain was immediately faced with economic and political turmoil. This period was known as the Age of Austerity. The national debt had risen substantially as Britain had spent close to seven billion pounds of the national wealth on the war effort. Large numbers of houses, factories and shops had been destroyed by bombings. Well over 300,000 military and civilian deaths left Britain with severe labour shortages, especially as those who survived were physically and mentally scarred by the war and mainly unable to return to normal life. The infrastructure of Britain had to be rebuilt and the country was in dire need of help. The *British Nationality Act 1948* granted the subjects of the British Empire the right to live and work in the UK and, in order to expedite the support Britain needed, they were not subject to immigration controls. It was during this time that the *HMT Empire Windrush* brought a group of 1,027 West Indian immigrants from Jamaica to London to aid in the recovery effort. The Windrush period represents the arrival of West Indian immigrants between 1948 and 1971 when an estimated 500,000 people came to live in the UK.

Although we hear mainly about the *Windrush* (the *HMT Empire Windrush*), it was not the first ship to bring immigrants from the West Indies into Britain. In March 1947, the *SS Ormonde* brought 108 men from Jamaica to Liverpool and in December 1947, *HMS Almanzora* transported 200 West Indians to the port of Southampton. Two days after the *Windrush* docked in June 1948, 11 Labour MPs wrote to the then Prime Minister, Clement Atlee, calling for a stop to the "influx of coloured people" coming into Britain, despite these "coloured people" being invited to help to rebuild post-war Britain. Interestingly, the arrival of the immigrants both baffled and surprised British society as the men were dressed in expensive suits and were very well presented. The *Daily Mirror* news article of June 23, 1948, read: "There were even emigrants wearing zoot-style suits – very long-waisted jackets, big padded shoulders, slit pockets and peg-top trousers – costing £15 to £20". Oswald M. Denniston, a newly arrived Jamaican immigrant, explained to the reporter at the time that while a number of the people who came were jobseekers, there were others that had come to Britain to finish their education. He also explained that poverty was not the reason he had come to Britain. I imagine this must have been hard to swallow for people in Britain who have always been led to believe the worst of black people. I don't suppose these fine gentlemen looked like the criminals and savages the British public was expecting to see.

These immigrants were British subjects who had proudly come to do their duty and they all experienced racism and discrimination. Racial attacks were widespread, and they found it difficult to get housing and were generally treated with hostility by companies who did not want to hire black people. Black children were bullied and mistreated in school by white children and this behaviour appeared to be generally condoned by parents and teachers. Teachers deliberately assessed black children as needing to be in remedial learning facilities purely on a racial bias and purposely misled West Indian parents into thinking that these facilities were exclusive and special for their children's needs. Racism in education was born at this point in Britain and then embedded in systems to support the "West Indian child becoming educationally sub-normal in the British school system" (Coard, 1971).

37

THE SPACE FOR STRUCTURAL CHANGE – VISIBLE

Questions for reflection:

1   How can early years education settings ensure that the legacy of making the West Indian child "educationally sub-normal" in the British school system is not a part of the unseen curriculum?

Despite the trauma of the experiences of the Windrush generation, we have to bear in mind that this was a time of the expansion of the concept of what it meant to be British. It is sometimes easy to forget that Caribbean communities were already very diverse with cultural influences from Latin America, Africa, and Asia. Think of the impact this had on music, for example. Areas in the country, especially London, experienced a fusion of music influences, which evolved and exist to this day. I have white friends, in my age group, who put me to shame with their reggae and salsa moves. The legacy continues on TikTok, where past and current Caribbean music styles are being mastered by dancers of all ages. We can't ignore the influences of Caribbean fashion, food, and vibrancy that have also infused British society. Alongside the trauma is the resilience and revolutionary behaviour of Caribbean people, so while we speak about how Britain positively influenced the physical infrastructure of the Caribbean, we can also explore how the Caribbean has influenced Britain in positive ways, including re-energising a flagging economy.

The first half of the 21st century – "Here we are!": the age of confusion, contradiction, and contestation

In our most recent history, we appear to be in denial about systemic racism, despite evidence to the contrary. A clear example is the recent experience of the Windrush generation, who in 2012, after changes to the immigration laws, were told they needed official documents to prove that they had a right to be in Britain and to receive the benefits due to citizens of this country despite the well-documented conditions under which they had entered the UK in the first place and all that they had done to rebuild Britain. This led to West Indian people who had lived in Britain for decades being sent to detention centres and, in some cases, deported, in what is now referred to as the Windrush scandal. In April 2018, the UK government apologised for the scandal and in April 2019 the Windrush compensation scheme was established, with some 15,000 people being eligible for compensation. Many of the people affected do not trust the Home Office, and this makes them afraid to apply for compensation. So far, only 3,000 people have claimed, and only around 750 people have received compensation.

When slave owners were being compensated for their "properties" which they lost due to the abolition of slavery, the British Government borrowed £20 million and made these payments swiftly. At that point, the compensation loan represented an enormous 40 per cent of the Treasury's annual income. British taxpayers would have remained blissfully unaware of this arrangement if someone had not posted the celebration of the last loan repayment in 2015 on Twitter. *2015! Only seven years ago!* Imagine, as a black person, discovering in 2015 that my hard-earned money was being used to repay slave owners! It is sad to note that compensation seemed to be quite a simple, straightforward process for slave owners but is not so for the victims of racism and discrimination. Racism is still a powerful force in modern British life, and it affects the lives of *all* British citizens in some way. All social systems including education are shaped by the legacies of slavery and continue to affect the translation of policies and practices in various ways, for communities who are disproportionately affected. We only need look at recent public health disasters such as the Grenfell Tower Fire in 2017 to understand the far-reaching impact of continued "inaction in the face of need" and how this affects poorer and ethnic minority communities. It is reported that 75 people died in the Grenfell fire, 57 of whom were from black and ethnic minority communities and 18 of whom were young children.

Truly understanding British history is an important part of the journey towards a more equitable society for all. Fowler (2020) explains that "A nation that doesn't understand its own history and the roots of its wealth will struggle to understand how power, finance, politics and economies work", especially, I believe, to uphold white supremacy and systemic racism. She argues that a nation that doesn't understand its past can't understand its present, and will struggle to understand how the legacy of slavery and empire remain at the heart of British life today. Some of our families were enriched by it, and some of our families were impoverished and brutalised by it.

She concretes this argument by saying that the legacy of slavery "is alive in almost every aspect of modern British life you care to name" (Fowler, 2020), which appears to be a concept that is very hard accept in modern Britain.

THE SPACE FOR TRANSFORMATIVE CHANGE – INVISIBLE

Safe space activity:

1. How am I personally affected by this history and its implications?
2. Slavery happened a long time ago Why is it necessary to dredge up all of this?
3. How will change affect me? Do I really want to change? What will be the impact on my friends and family if I change?
4. What if I believe that children will not be any worse off if things remain the same?
5. Discuss why black parents' own early years experiences may produce a lack of trust in early years experiences for their children.

"The Water of Systems Change" reminds us to focus on the invisible, which my 93-year-old aunt reminded me of in a recent conversation. She told me some truths that deviated from the normal stories of the time; she told me about the kindness of strangers in a hostile 1950s Britain. These people were not perfect nor were they politically correct, but they were genuine. My Aunt Pearl came to live in Britain in 1950; she arrived on the *Reina del Pacifico*, which was an ocean liner cruise ship. Although she was working in the NHS at the time, she was facing extreme racism and was struggling. She was fortunate enough through family contacts to be invited to live with a British family to look after their child for one night a week to enable the wife and husband to go out for the evening. She reports having a large room all to herself and being treated with kindness. She was given extra blankets and the fire was put on every evening so that she wasn't cold. She also spoke about "Nan", a woman my aunt met when she was pushing her baby in her "pram" in Forest Hills, South East London, on the long daily journey to where the baby was going to be looked after for the day before Nan went on to work. My aunt remembers how hard this was, especially in the winter months. Nan introduced herself to my aunt and, very soon after, expressed her longing to look after "a black baby", despite Nan's husband having serious concerns about his wife's wishes. Nan showed my Aunt Pearl more love as a mother than she had ever known, as Aunt Pearl's mother had died when she was a baby.

My aunt also told me of the experiences of racism her children had to go through in the education system, but she also spoke for ages about all the times Nan stood up for her and my cousins. There are many more stories like this that need to be told to remind us of humanity in action, because only love and compassion can loosen the stranglehold of hate and fear. People like Nan were changemakers! She had not studied the art or science of changemaking, but it was in her DNA. Maybe that will be my next project. Many of my aunt's friends have died holding on to these stories of ordinary British people who showed extraordinary kindness in a hostile situation; people who stood out from the crowd, despite the culture of their country. People like this, people who make up their own minds and follow their heart, exist today. As early years professionals there is a need for us to stand out from the crowd, just like these unsung heroes. The tide of the vast ocean can turn just from the ripple of our little pond in the early years.

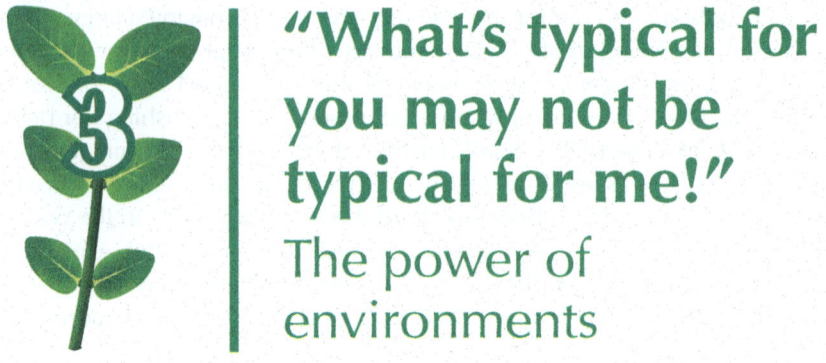

"What's typical for you may not be typical for me!"
The power of environments

The earliest years of childhood is a time when the greatest opportunities for healthy development are most active and, as with other things, the greatest opportunities usually present openings for the greatest risks as well. We mentioned brain function in Chapter 1 but let us revisit brain development from an early childhood perspective. The early years are a period of rapid brain development; 90 per cent of a child's brain develops by the time they are five years old. Brain development in young children during this time is also susceptible to toxic stress, and research also tells us that it is difficult for children to make the most of their learning environments if:

- They have challenging home environments.
- They have poor-quality early childhood services.
- They have poor-quality community and social environments.

The experiences and relationships that young children have contribute to brain development and also build the neural circuits that will form the foundation for later development. Children's brains are therefore being actively constructed in the moment, as they connect and interact with their environments. I will try to categorise the environments that children should encounter to promote the desired theoretical standards for healthy childhood development (Diagram 3.1).

Desired outcomes for children are set against ideal standards and the associated evaluation of traits and attributes that are perfect for meeting these standards. However, real life always gets in the way, and desired outcomes

DOI: 10.4324/9781003247807-3

Diagram 3.1 Desired outcomes for children.

Environments	Desired outcomes
• **Physical** – home/housing/family life • **Service** – childcare and education/ academic and non-academic/learning, health care/leisure • **Social** – community life/community services/culture/race/social status/ gender/immigration status • **Economic** – employment/low or no family income	• Appropriate investments in healthy child development by parents, teachers, practitioners, health and social care professionals, policy-makers, researchers • Interconnected positive outcomes across diverse domains of child-development
Environments that nurture caring and wellbeing as well as physical health and safety	Positive wellbeing and secure attachments Healthy physical development Safeguarding and child welfare **(Physical health and safety are fundamental for achieving other desired outcomes)**
Environments that nurture emotional and behavioural competence	Positive emotional and mental health A sense of security Self-regulation and independence
Environments that nurture social competence	Basic social skills – empathy, co-operation, sharing – skills associated with future success in school, work, and family life
Environments that nurture cognitive competence	Stimulating, challenging, supportive learning environments Skills and capacities needed at each age and stage of development Cognitive competence in language and communication, reading, writing, mathematics, problem-solving

for children have to be based in their resilience to navigate, accommodate and compensate for whatever life throws at them. Most people want the best for their children and people who are able to operationalise consistency in their social circumstances are generally quite successful in achieving the best for their children, in essence, achieving the "typical pattern of early childhood development".

However, ideal standards can be a source of never-ending strife for families who are marginalised, families who live with poverty and deprivation, families who may have children with special needs and medical issues, families who experience life-changing emotional distress such as death and divorce; this is where our expertise as early years practitioners comes into play. It may be important for us to rethink, reframe, and reconstruct "ideal standards" against a more diverse social framework in order even to begin to make a difference for *all* children.

THE SPACE FOR STRUCTURAL CHANGE – VISIBLE

Questions for reflection:

1. Based on Diagram 3.1, how can we ensure that the ethos, philosophy, and pedagogy in our learning environments in the early years nurture the:
    o   Care, wellbeing and physical health and safety of all involved in the learning community?
    o   Emotional and behavioural competence for everyone?
    o   Social competence of all children to ensure that they are ready for their academic journeys?
    o   Cognitive competence that stimulates, challenges, and supports each child to their full academic potential?

I am always fascinated by the nostalgia surrounding "traditional" families. I hear so many people bemoaning the loss of the traditional family, the apparent "breakdown of family life", and the complicated context of contemporary families. However, society's ideals have always been a mask for what really happens in family life. We don't need to search too deeply for an example of unconventional family life: Boris Johnson, our Prime Minister at the time of writing, is a prime example. The current broadened concept of family overrides those of race, social status, and class. It is everywhere! So why does the concept of family appear to be still so tightly linked with class, race, and morality when it applies to black families? The disdain for black single mothers and the perceptions of black absentee fathers is palpable in society, with blame being openly attributed to their class, race, and morality.

It seems to me that black families are being held to a far higher standard than someone like the Prime Minister of the United Kingdom!

If we can't relate to statistical data, we tend to reject the validity of the data but, for the most part, many people have a deep understanding of the complexity of the family as it reflects their reality and what they see around them in their communities. The OECD Better Life Initiative urges policy makers to "look beyond the functioning of the economic system to consider the diverse experiences and living conditions of people and households" (Durand, 2013). It has to be acknowledged that both socio-economic advantage and disadvantage manifests in very different ways across different ethnic groups in multicultural societies such as the UK. Below is an example of black family life in contemporary Britain. It is my hope that understanding this a bit more may help to level the playing field a bit for the black child and support the effectiveness of how we implement anti-racist practice in the early years.

Although Diagram 3.2 speaks the slightly dry language of sociological analysis in regard to the macro, meso, and micro levels surrounding black family life, these levels are generally useful in understanding the interrelationships that different levels of society have on family life in general. This type of analysis depicts how legal and policy systems, hierarchies, economies, and institutions shape the culture of our country right down to the specific aspects of social phenomena that impact on the black family. Each of these levels has an upward and downward flow that impacts on the levels below and above. The circumstances surrounding black families are reinforced and institutionalised as nationally influenced policies flow down and collide with the realities of black family life, creating and deepening a policy rut.

The meritocracy myth

Most of us have been led to believe that British culture is built on a meritocratic society where a person's progress, job, and pay are based on individual talent and achievement rather than on social status. The implications are that individuals who work hard will be rewarded, whilst those who do not, will not be rewarded. The problem is that while a meritocracy sounds reasonable in theory it does not translate smoothly into practice. If society is rife with inequality, how can it be meritocratic? For a start, money impacts the

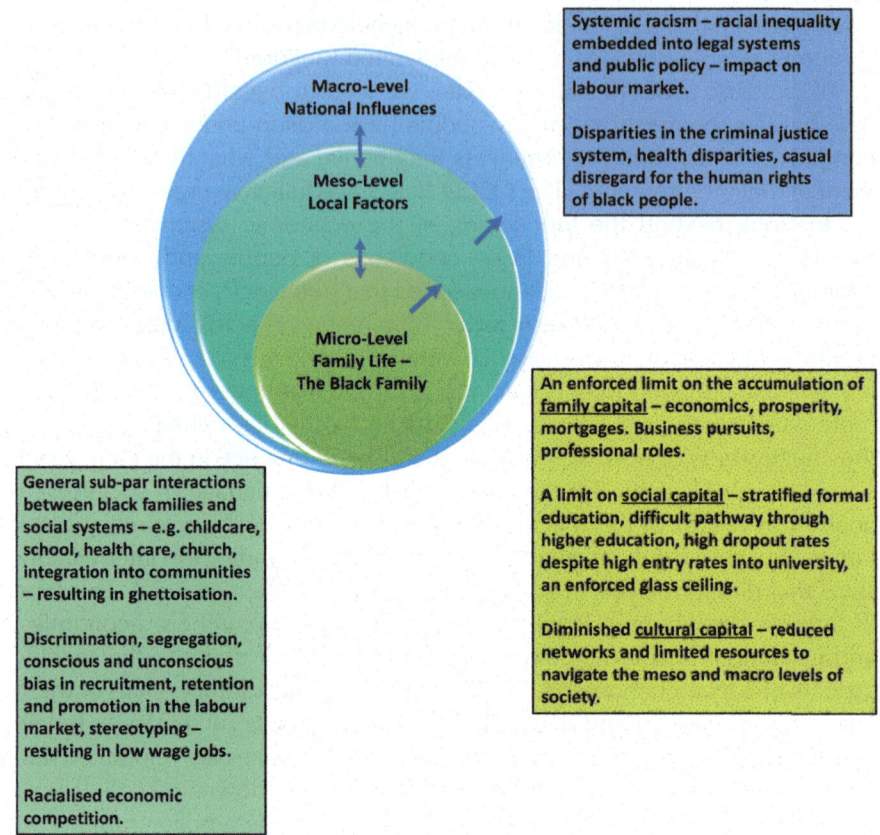

Diagram 3.2 The socio-ecological phenomenon of the black family in multicultural Britain.

quality of education and the opportunities associated with education. We live in a society where education is literally the best that money can buy! This is a stark reality in the early years in Britain. The wealthy spend huge amounts of money getting their children into the most prestigious nurseries in just the right locations. As we saw with the concept of ideal standards for desired outcomes, the world has a habit of creating perfect models to address our imperfect world. The idea that this country is meritocratic conflicts with the realities of certain members of our society, especially ethnic

'The world is just'

Adapted from (Berkley, 2016)
'Distributive Justice and Theories Wrap up'

Figure 3.1 Is the world just?

minority people and the poorer and oppressed in society. Their perspective is captured in the cartoon in Figure 3.1.

The concept of meritocracy is based on the idea that everyone has the same opportunities and the same access to resources and support, but the issue with this, evident in Figure 3.1, is that the greatest or the least benefit depends on where you are positioned in the hierarchy. If you are at the bottom of the hierarchy then not very much seems fair but if you are at the top, everything generally seems fair. If, as an early years practitioner, you truly believe that everyone has the same opportunities and the same access to success, then it would seem fair to assume that if black children do not succeed, then, logically, it would be because:

- They are genetically less intelligent and less able.
- Their parents are lazy and therefore not able to look after them or support them.
- If only they knew how to behave more like white people, they would not have as many problems as they do.

Unfortunately, black children and their families are often depicted as the problem and made to be hyper-visible as being "biologically inferior", while the circumstances and people who perpetuate racism remain invisible. Invisibility is a powerful asset, especially as it leaves most of us who are trying to make change struggling to explain why the version of fairness that embodies the power of the "white population", who found themselves in a position centuries ago to dictate whose life goes in which direction, is not inherently fair at all. Imagine how exhausting it is for black children to apparently be "objectively" labelled as less intelligent and less able, which then, of course, makes it perfectly natural for them to "reap what they sow". This means that practitioners who may consciously or unconsciously hold these beliefs, are automatically excused from responsibility for the poor outcomes of black children. How does the average black family climb this greasy pole? Generally not very well, I think, and definitely not without some bumps and bruises.

We know that environmental factors play a key role in early childhood inequality. If there is to be sustainable change, we have to consider whether everyone has access to, and receives, the same quality of education. Do we live in a society where there is inconsistency in educational outcomes? Does a lack of trust in social systems impact negatively on some community groups? These are questions that need to be thoroughly explored to implement the right kind of actions to reduce early childhood inequalities. Most black and ethnic minority adults born in the UK are born into a system that has always been unfairly stacked against them because of the persistent and pervasive ideology of biological superiority which is always at the heart of systemic racism.

Systemic racism creates a gap between communities of people who are hardwired not to trust each other's motives. So, sadly, trust is a casualty of systemic racism; the loss of trust in people and in public bodies who are publicly funded to support *all* citizens. This is a fact that has to be appreciated in the implementation of anti-racist practices. Despite our best intentions for the greater good, the journey will never be easy, especially as quite a bit of the challenge will come from the very same people who will benefit from anti-racist practice, due to this ingrained lack of trust.

"But I didn't mean any harm!"

Most of the majority population in Britain are generally not equipped to identify the subtler forms of systemic racism and can usually only relate to it if there is the forceful presence of vicious intent in the interaction. This means that the impact of experiences of racism are relegated to being subjective and are not regarded as sufficient to bring about widespread systemic changes because there is no perceived intention of racial harm. In my 43 years of practice in education, I have come across many situations where there was no *intent* to harm a child but the outcome of the person's actions still resulted in harm for that child.

I will give you an example from my experience as a young teacher at the age of 19. I had fairly long nails and I took pride in keeping them looking nice. I remember a specific occasion when my class of three-year-olds and myself were acting out a story during story time. I was in my element, performing my part using vigorous and exaggerated arm gestures when a little girl suddenly stepped up behind me and my nail went directly into her eye, and I actually scratched the cornea in her eye. I had no intent of harm, so by following the logic of "no intent to harm", I could just have made excuses and blamed that child for moving into my space unexpectedly; or, I had a duty to recognise that any child aged three is unpredictable at the best of times and I needed to cut my nails to reduce the possibility of an accident like this happening again, which is what I did.

No intent to harm cannot excuse the actual ongoing harm being perpetuated on black and ethnic minority children. While restaurateurs may have no intent to give their diners a salmonella infection, immediate action is always taken to address the issue in the best interest of the public. Salmonella may last for up to seven days in your system and it is the worst! Diarrhoea, vomiting, fever, and abdominal cramps. Now imagine that these severe symptoms were medically apparent in all the people who suffer racism, but the symptoms are ongoing and never-ending. Racism is societal salmonella.

THE SPACE FOR TRANSFORMATIVE CHANGE – INVISIBLE

Questions for reflection:

1. Do you instinctively perceive some children to be more capable than others on sight? What do you think might be the cause of this?
2. Do we believe that the circumstances of children and families predestine their outcomes? How might this impact on the way we interact with children?
3. What are the stereotypes that are attributed to black people? How might these affect how you interact with black children?

"But you have done quite well as a black woman the UK, so it can't be all that bad"

At this point I am usually accused of hypocrisy because to all intents and purposes I have been successful in this very same system that I say is systemically racist and, of course, there are a number of notable, successful black and ethnic minority people living in the UK. Just a quick reminder that I did not grow up in the UK, but trust me when I say that successful black people have a story to tell! They will have stories of defying the system; stories of conforming to the point of denying themselves; stories of being in the right place at the right time; stories of being "exceptionalised" when their abilities could not be easily excused away; stories of rare cases of black role models who appeared in their lives, who inspired or supported their success; stories of creating their own pathway to success; or stories like Ian Wright's, of an amazing teacher who saw past skin colour in his career as a teacher and was "irrationally crazy" about all his students and just as equally invested in all of their successes. What they generally will not have had is a smooth rite of passage, that is:

Good student = Good university = Good career = Successful life.

Being successful as a black person entails being equipped to continually break through a series of glass, sometimes concrete, ceilings that randomly appear above you. Allow me to be frank: as a black professional woman, this does not in any way translate to a comfortable seat at the table of success. This space, in my own personal experience, becomes open season for all the negative tropes attributed to successful black women – loud, aggressive, opinionated, formidable, scary, ghetto, are a few that spring to mind, plus the stereotypical musings of being hired to fill a quota along with being over-scrutinised in work practice as if somehow being black is synonymous with being dishonest or incapable. To add insult to injury, the habit of unfairly rolling out successful black men and women in public as an example of what black people can achieve "if only they worked harder" only provides the escape route society needs in order to remain in a place of apathy and never address what it takes for black children, from as young as their early years, to battle to become successful men and women in UK society. This is the life young black children have to continue to look forward to if nothing changes.

Marmot (2010) had six recommendations in his "Fair Society, Healthy Lives" review; the highest priority recommendation was: "Give every child the best start in life" (p. 14). In assessing anti-racist practice in the early years, we can never underestimate the power of the environments we operate in, in our quest to give each child the best start in life. Bronfenbrenner (1979) embodies the idea of giving children the best start in life. He heavily supports the fact that children who are socialised in childhood trauma often experience emotional and behavioural problems; but he never diagnosed these problems as problems with the children but rather as problems with the ecology in which the child exists and with the deep contrasts between a healthy ecology and a high-risk ecology for children. Children who experience conscious and unconscious racism exist in a perpetual high-risk ecology and I suggest that we, as practitioners, have to cultivate an understanding of systemic racism as a high-risk ecology before labelling and writing-off young black children.

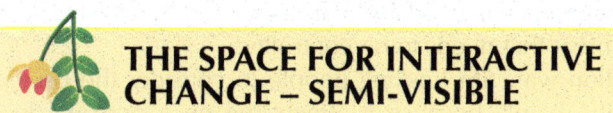

THE SPACE FOR INTERACTIVE CHANGE – SEMI-VISIBLE

Questions for reflection:

1. How can we rationally assess if we are giving *every* child the best start in life in our settings?
2. Based on the views of Bronfenbrenner, how can we tell if the circle of influence we have in the early years creates stress or offers support for the child?
3. How might dual-heritage children's experience of the world around them impact on their wellbeing during the early years?

If, somewhere in the recesses of our minds, we feel even a tiny bit of relief about not having to worry about the colour of our skin, then is it possible to imagine standing in the place of the people who do have to worry about the colour of their skin? My beautiful five-year-old granddaughter told me recently that she wished she had skin like her mummy. This is a little girl who has positive role models in her life, a well-educated family who values both of her cultural heritages. She is fortunate enough to have solid reserves of family capital, social capital, and cultural capital from having professional parents and from being my only grandchild; still yet, through no fault of her own, she has absorbed society's ideals that being white is better than being who she is. This makes me very sad.

Swimming against the tide

A true commitment to anti-racist practice can feel like swimming against the tide as it constitutes intentional behaviour that is contrary to widely held social beliefs. There were a couple of hard questions that I had to ask myself as part of doing this project, the first question being: if the tables were turned would I be so concerned about inequality? I would like to think that I would, but the honest answer is that I really don't know. Suffice it to say that I do not in any way underestimate the hurdles that need to be leapt to implement anti-racist practice in the early years especially as equality is usually perceived as a threat that needs to be controlled.

The other question was: am I asking people to consider the issues of racism and inequality mainly because it affects me on a personal level? The answer to that is two-fold – yes, because I would like to see change during my lifetime, so as to be able to envision a more equitable future for my children and grandchildren and a future where children of colour are comfortable just being themselves. But even more importantly, research tells us that inequality affects us all negatively even if and when we benefit from an unequal society. Inequality leads to wasted productive potential which in turn leads to an inefficient allocation of resources (World Bank, 2013, p. 29). The vast differences in education, health and nutrition in marginalised communities results in low educational attainment, high unemployment rates, poor living conditions, and high poverty rates. This ultimately creates a drain on public resources and private investments. Resources are not infinite, so inequality has an adverse effect on *all* in society. Evidence gathered by Wilkinson and Pickett (2009) shows that more unequal societies experience more social and environmental problems across the whole population than more equal societies.

There are a number of people reading this who may be having a gut reaction, especially if they genuinely perceive themselves to be non-racist and even anti-racist. There are people who will wholeheartedly say "I do not see race" or "I do not see colour, all I see are people"; while this sounds idyllic, please spare a thought for the black mother or father who has no choice but to see and understand that colour matters so that they are able to prepare their child for a world that will more than likely treat them unfairly. Let us bring on a world that actively promotes nurturing environments and the associated desired outcomes for *all* children.

THE SPACE FOR TRANSFORMATIVE CHANGE – INVISIBLE

Questions for reflection:

1   What are the implications of the concept of a "colour-blind" learning environment for children?
2   What is the difference between being non-racist and being anti-racist?

"Are we really that different?"

Debunking stereotypical perceptions and popular myths

The poem "Really," was written for me by my Twitter friend, Charles Dale, "the Lockdown Laureate." If he sounds familiar, that's because you may have come across him in his other role as an actor in TV series such as *Coronation Street* and *Casualty*. I have never actually met Charles, but this poem is a little bit like my claim to fame! The spoken version on Twitter and YouTube starts off like this: "Hello Dr Val, this is for you, do with it what you may." Dr Val! That's me! (I can see my sons visibly shrinking.) Well, Charles, thank you for taking up my challenge. Your poem speaks to the heart of stereotypical perceptions. To all my readers, I sincerely hope this poem gives you food for thought and that it makes some points worthy of being mulled over and discussed. You can watch the powerful spoken version on: https://youtu.be /m_S-_8JxY-k.

Although it's easy to think that children in the early years are protected from these stereotypes, let us have a look at how they permeate the lives of the youngest in society? Based on how prejudicial attitudes are reproduced in society, when we meet our new cohort of children for the year, from just looking at them, have we already decided:

- Who will require most of our attention?
- Who is able and who is not?
- Who is poor and who is not?
- Who comes from a good family and who does not?

Is there a possibility that we may treat children deferentially according to our preconceived beliefs? There is a dire need for accurate, culturally aware

DOI: 10.4324/9781003247807-4

representation of black people and their lives in the UK, but this need constantly battles with a longstanding historical resistance to hearing the stories of black communities from actual black people. Instead, our stories are often told for us generally, with quite a bit of indifference to cultural nuances and routinely from an analytical standpoint of how black communities deplete and diminish British culture and British public funds. Who wouldn't be annoyed at that? In fact, it has taken a significant amount of time and effort for me to understand that all is not as it seems, and that is speaking as a black woman and an academic. I find myself asking how to embed the need for practitioners to sift through the rubble of stereotypes to get to the real underpinning issues surrounding the lives of black children in the early years. As educators we have to remember that the way we treat young children has deep repercussions for how they see themselves and what they believe about themselves. These beliefs stay with young children from their early years and sometimes for the rest of their lives.

"Who are they trying to fool?"

Black Britishness in the UK is generally viewed through the lens of white Britishness, as was apparent in the outrage of the general British public over a Christmas advert that depicted a black family doing normal things at Christmas. This, in my opinion, is a symptom of the vast misrepresentation of black family life. I have to admit that I was unclear about what the real issue was for those who had such a visceral reaction and perhaps this is something we can talk about together to inform ourselves. From a place where I am making assumptions, I struggle to find any imaginable reasoning beyond:

- The British public may not want to see black families on their TV screens; or,
- The British public may not want to see black families depicted in a human way; or,
- The British public may not want to believe that black family life is not that different to white family life.

After assessing this whole issue against brain function and the response of the amygdala when we see someone different to us, and also what might hinder the effectiveness of the prefrontal cortex in regulating and calming down the amygdala, it dawned on me that the general public is probably just more comfortable with people who they feel connected to as part of their "in-group." As controversial as this reasoning may seem, I was aiming to see this issue as coming from a subconscious level, which does not sub-scribe to social convention. Ideally, I would want this ad to be enjoyed by all as unremarkably British – a society accepting of diverse family lives – but, sadly, I know that the social construction of black people in the mindset of the general public is historical, negative, and pervasive. The usual response I have encountered is "At least it is not as bad as in America and other places in the world." This is a fair point, but it does fall a bit flat for the people who experience racism as a daily part of life. Degrees of racism, in my mind, is a bit like saying "Well, I am pregnant but only a little bit pregnant, so it doesn't really count." Perhaps being locked into our roles as educators and practitioners when our subconscious is operating without mindfulness of unconscious bias may help to explain some of the disparities in education for ethnic minority children. Shand-Baptiste (2020) informs us that "these are disparities that exist not because of any underlying propensity to cause trouble, but probably because educators perceive black children as funda-mentally disruptive, hopeless, and inferior, regardless of what they do."

Think about what is promoted about black people and their lives in the UK. Does it look something like Diagram 4.1, and have we taken measures to recognise when ideas like these seep into our practice?

Sadly, for any family, despite race, a number of the "labels" above in the grid may be true but if the assumption is that these "labels" are photo-stamped on to the lives of all black children, then the sad fallout is that black children may be treated as a standardised group of delinquents who are not deserving of any real time and effort as it will all just be wasted anyway. What is truly sad is that the persistence of these perceptions in the UK blinds the observer to the true circumstances of diverse black family life whereas the diverse circumstances of white family life is understood and accommo-dated. Unconsciously selective aspirations for the children in our care can result in an almost natural promotion of "good enough" but not the best, due to an unspoken but widely accepted culture that expects underachievement from black children. The subtleness of a teaching and learning culture where you unconsciously do your best for children who look like you or are from similar backgrounds as yourself may inadvertently impact on the time and

Diagram 4.1 Perceptions of black people and their families.

Black people are lazy and abuse the system	Thugs Animals Ghetto Gangster	Single mothers Different fathers Loud women Left a bunch of children behind in their country
Absentee fathers Dads in jail Criminals – thieves, rapists, murderers	Selling/buying/using drugs Love to party, hate to work	Look weird Dress weird Smell weird Speak weird Act weird Eat weird food **They are not like normal people!**
Beat their children Violent Social services involvement	Unintelligent Illiterate Barely able to speak English	Poor backgrounds/came here for a better life "Bolshie" Scary Promiscuous Dysfunctional family life

energy that is spent on the majority of ethnic minority children. I am of the school of thought that high standards in our profession as early years practitioners must include conscious anti-racist practice.

THE SPACE FOR TRANSFORMATIVE CHANGE – INVISIBLE

Questions for reflection:

1. Why might black children be unhappy in their settings?
2. How much control do we as leaders and practitioners have over how children view their experience in their learning environments?
3. Why should leaders and practitioners be expected to ensure that all children have an equitable experience in their learning environments?

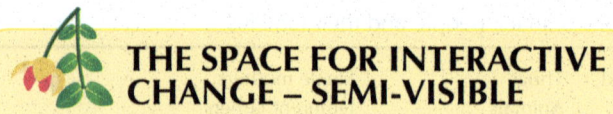

THE SPACE FOR INTERACTIVE CHANGE – SEMI-VISIBLE

Questions for reflection:

1. What would be involved in delivering a broader and richer curriculum?
2. What measures could we take to ensure that our curriculum is representative and inclusive?
3. How can we identify and eradicate what is perceived as an attitude of indifference and incidents of discriminatory practice towards children and parents?

"Not everything is about race! Why do we never talk about class?"

There is a long history in the UK of reviewing the "failures of the black family" outside of the context of racial disadvantage. There also appears to be a resistance to focus too deeply on the systemic structures that create, promote, and reinforce these stereotypes in the first place and how they then become embedded in the minds of the average citizen and, without a doubt, in the minds of young children. Read about Matty and his friend.

CASE STUDY 2: THE EXPERIENCES OF THE "PROFESSIONAL" BLACK FAMILY

Matty and his friend

I don't mind admitting that this case study is about my younger son, Matty. He was seven years old and had just brought his first friend over for tea since moving from London to Birmingham. I was excited for him as he had been missing his friends that he had left behind in London. Well, this cute little girl with a long blond ponytail runs into my house, then proceeds to walk around my house and garden with a startled expression on her face, and her parents, coming in behind her, were barely managing to conceal their surprise. Sadly, I was quite used to that reaction. Matty in the meantime was running behind his friend, trying to get her to play, but she was having none of it. I was carrying a tray with hot drinks and snacks into the living room where my husband was entertaining the girl's parents, when this little girl accosts me with this question: "I just want to know how *you* can afford a house like this?" The emphasis on the "*you*" was deliberate and emphatic. Her parents called out to her in shame, telling her that what she said was rude, but I decided to answer her anyway. "We are both working professionals, just like your mum and dad." She responded: "Well my mum is a solicitor, and we can't afford a house like this!" My response was "But we can!" At this point I realised I was trying to justify myself to a seven-year-old who could only have been the mouthpiece of her parent's attitudes towards black people. They were sitting, red-faced, choking down the tea and snacks, looking really uncomfortable while their little girl was standing with her arms folded across her chest, decidedly disgruntled that we lived in a nice house, with a nice garden, and drove nice cars. I have never forgotten this. I realised then and there that we were a bit of a social experiment for this family; they had accepted my son's invitation expecting to come into a scenario that looked more like the grid in Diagram 4.1, but I was seriously gobsmacked about how much prejudice their seven-year-old daughter had subsumed from her family life at such a young age.

THE SPACE FOR TRANSFORMATIVE CHANGE – INVISIBLE

Questions for reflection:

1. Think about a time in your setting when you were truly surprised that your perception of a child did not match with who the child really was at all.

2. Discuss why it may be easier to exceptionalise these surprising situations as one-offs if it applies to black children and still cling to negative stereotypes.

THE SPACE FOR STRUCTURAL CHANGE – VISIBLE

Questions for reflection:

1. Think about a time in your setting when a child said something racist to another child. How did that make you feel? How was the situation handled? What policies are in place to handle these incidents?

The case study above shows the persistence of stereotyping; even when black people work hard and are successful, they are still treated with either anger or suspicion for what they have achieved and, unfortunately, black parents can only partially protect their children from the long arm of racism and prejudice. Prejudice means that consciously or unconsciously, a decision has already been made and this decision results in being disinclined to look deeper or further because of the perceived certainty of "knowing what you know." Eckhart Tolle refers to this as being "identified with the mind"; "identification with your mind creates an opaque screen of concepts, labels, images, words, judgements, and definitions that block all true relationships" (Tolle 2004, p. 15).

Matty's life was totally natural to him as a black child; he had no sense of inferiority or superiority, just a sense of security. Matty is my younger son, and he is blessed with loads of natural emotional intelligence; his favourite comment when he was little was "When you look deep to it mummy," which he frequently used to describe something that he had experienced on the surface and then what he felt was the deeper meaning of that experience. Still, he was totally unaware of any social difference between himself and his friend. I spoke to him about this event recently and he told me that having grown up in London up till this point, race seemed to be less of a topic, and back in London he had friends of all races; so while he thought his friend's behaviour was odd, he hadn't really understood why. The concept of a black middle-class family was jarring for my son's guests and, to be fair, it is a concept that does not sit comfortably in British society – not even with black middle-class parents who prefer to be identified as "professional" rather than middle-class, according to Vincent et al. (2012). This piece of research resonated with me for a number of reasons as they found that:

- Racism is a reality in the lives of black middle-class families.
- Black parents recognise racism as "pervasive in more subtle and coded forms affecting them and their children."
- Black middle-class parents have to be vigilant to protect their children from racist incidents and the effects of racism in school life.
- Because of white society's denial of racism, black professional parents rarely make explicit mention of racism as a barrier to their children's educational success, even when there is clear evidence to uphold this assertion. "Experience tells them that the term 'racism' is likely to be met with resistance and antagonism by teachers, tutors and school staff."

The summary of this research explained that while black professional parents use aspects of their class advantage to mitigate the effects of racism, their social class does not shield them from racism. The report highlighted low expectations from teachers for black children and the extra work that needed to be put in by black middle-class parents for them to be taken seriously by white teachers and staff in learning environments. Professional black parents are privileged in that they can, more than likely, make time to be vigilant in their children's education; way more than a working-class black family may be able to, for various reasons. I thought long and hard about this summary and how hands-on I am as a parent. When I think of my older son between 18 months and five years old, this phrase comes to mind: "But why mummy?" Being around him was intense because he spoke really well from very early on and he had no interest in toys, just an insatiable interest in how things worked and why things were the way they were. His poor childminder, who had him from he was a one-year-old, found it difficult to give him the attention he demanded and also look after the other children in her care so she suggested that my son should go to a playgroup that was run by her two friends who, coincidentally, both had their children in my reception class in the primary school where I taught. John would be the youngest in the playgroup at 18 months, but they would see how he got on. So, story time on my son's first day and how the playgroup experience unfolded.

STORY TIME: JOHN'S (18 MONTHS) PLAYGROUP EXPERIENCE

Me: Did you like your first day in school? [I called it school because it made him feel important.]

John: Yes, but I am not going back.

Me: WHY? What happened?

John: She gave me the hat, then they wanted to take away my hat and I said no! So they said I was naughty and they told me to pick up the toys the other children were playing with and I said no because I wasn't being naughty, it was my hat! They took my hat mummy!

Me: Huh! Ok, never mind, I will come with you tomorrow and we will speak to Kate.

I asked my headteacher if I could get into work a bit later and went to drop John off the next morning. I asked Kate what had happened the day before and she told me John had a lovely time in playgroup. I told her that he had not wanted to come in because someone had taken his hat. Kate was standing there with her mouth open looking at John and looking at me. She said, "John told you this?" I really wanted to say, "Well how else would I know this, because all you have just said is that he had a lovely day yesterday," but I was polite and just said "Yes." Kate explained that they give children hats for sand play to stop sand getting into their hair but when they tried to put away the hats at tidy-up time, John refused to take off the hat and just kept shouting "No" whenever they tried to take it from him. They eventually took it from him and told him to tidy up and he refused to help. I asked if she had explained to him that the hat was only for sand play. Kate said she had not and that she had never had to do that with any other child before. I explained that John thought she had given him the hat for keeps and then was taking it away from him. I also explained that he thought she was telling him to tidy up as a punishment for not giving back the hat. By this time Kate was really flustered: "But he is only 18 months old!" I agreed with her and said that as he was the youngest child in the playgroup, he probably did not understand the rules. Kate said to me, "No! Not that! I can't believe *he* told you all of this. He didn't speak very much yesterday."

Fast forward three weeks, and my child is bouncing off the walls! And he is constantly telling me stories about his friend Amari who is the only other black child in the playgroup. "Amari was crying today because he got told off. He hit Emily but Emily hit him first! That's not fair, is it mummy?" I lost count of the sad stories about Amari and my hackles were up in case these two little black boys were receiving unfair treatment in the playgroup, so I asked John what he got told off for. "I don't get told off mummy. I am a good boy!" My thought at this point was, "Really John! You never get told off?" John has always been a purposeful and logical child and also very energetic.

As his mum I was tuned into asking him about the logic behind his actions, which meant that I had a better understanding of why behaviour that might look to be naughty was sometimes not; for example, taking loads of grass into the childminder's house into a corner she had set up as a vet's clinic. I pulled up after work to a very upset childminder who was not looking forward to cleaning all that grass out of her house, and an even more upset child. I asked him why he had done it and his response was, "The animals were in the vet all day mummy, and no one gave them any food so I gave them some food." The childminder was amazing; she told him that he was right and asked him to come with her to find a tray to put the grass in for the animals. However, and this links back to the playgroup part of the story, at this point I knew the behaviour he was displaying was more about testing boundaries and was not the normal run-of-the mill John behaviour. I asked the childminder if she was experiencing the same, to which she said she was, so I asked her to check in at the playgroup. It turns out that they were really uncomfortable with John's ability to express himself clearly and the fact that they knew that I, as a parent (the word "black" was not used but it certainly felt like it was floating around in the ether), would come in to check on his story. They basically just left him to run wild, especially because they had children in my class as well and they were worried that I might "take it out on them." A thought which had never crossed my mind! I took him out of the playgroup, but I always wondered if they realised that he told me many other stories which were not about him and were far more concerning, because even from a very young age John was always obsessed with fairness.

We know, as practitioners, that young children care passionately about justice and fairness for themselves and for others. Contrary to popular opinion, children are not "too small to notice" when things are not fair, even if it is unconscious behaviour on the part of an adult. Sadly, it is very common for children who have concerns about fairness to either be ignored or dismissed as being too small to really understand, especially when it comes to complaints against an adult. I note that one of the concerns the playgroup owners had was the fact that I listened to my son and took time to come in and follow up with them about his concerns. It is clear that Amari's mum either did not know how sad her son was, did not have the capacity to come in to follow up, or was resigned to thinking that this is the way things are, so no point creating a fuss.

When we perceive our subjective experiences as the only way of interpreting the world around us, we often forgo deeper and wider understanding. Aspiring to anti-racist practice means we have to be mindful of an ecology that almost casually perpetuates the implicit message that injustice directed towards young black children is somehow acceptable if there is no racial intent or if behaviour that comes naturally to a practitioner is lacking an awareness of unfairness.

THE SPACE FOR TRANSFORMATIVE CHANGE – INVISIBLE

Questions for reflection:

1. Think about a time in your setting when the staff have all agreed that an ethnic minority parent was "difficult." Discuss what the issues may have been for this parent.

"I know you are up to no good, I know about your kind!"

As educators, when we consciously or unconsciously operate from what we *think* we know, we are doing children a disservice that could and, in most cases, will have severe implications for the life of the child, way into adulthood. Prejudicial assumptions lead to:

- Misaligned resources – therefore wasted resources (in this current climate when people are losing jobs, can we continue to waste resources?).
- Discrimination.
- Pre-judgements of a child's capability as a learner.
- Deterioration of academic performance.
- Potentially missing what *all* children may need to thrive. (This works both ways: the child whose needs have been wrongly assessed based on stereotypical prejudice and also the child who is crying out for help that they may not receive because they are seen as white, middle-class, conventionally pretty/beautiful, etc. – in essence, from a "nice" family so they couldn't possibly be in need. This is then treated as a mere misunderstanding that just needs to be squared away, to the detriment of a child's wellbeing while insignificant and explainable issues for a black family could, in a lot of cases, be escalated disproportionately in another kind of detriment to the wellbeing of that child. The pendulum swings both ways! Educators who never question their stereotypical assumptions have unknowingly lost the capacity to just trust their gut and follow process.)

Stereotyping anyone is usually a way of putting them "in their place" and fixing them there. Defining an individual primarily in terms of their visual ethnic identity is actually a way of defining them as "different" from a "white standard," and playing down any similarities with other human beings. If we normalise attributing qualities to people based on their supposed "differences" from an imagined "white standard" then this tends to allow for sweeping generalisations. People who are categorised according to difference are then not seen for who they are on an individual basis but rather on widely shared assumptions about belonging to a specific group. We can link this back to the "in-group"–"out-group" mentality, especially if it is allowed to run free and unchecked in our minds. Sadly, generalisations are usually negative and reflect existing patterns of racism in society – and at the same time they help to perpetuate racism because stereotyping people with fixed negative attributes both reflects and reproduces inequality. "Racism in nurseries: 'Black babies hardly picked up and left in dirty nappies for hours'" (Albert, 2021, Daynurseries .co.uk) is an article specifically about racism in the early years and it highlights these issues:

- Three-year-olds hearing negative comments about their skin colour.
- A lack of attention, care, and warmth.
- Only two per cent of books published in the UK featured a black main character in 2019, according to the Office for National Statistics.
- Nursery staff smiling and being pleasant with white parents but displaying a distinct shift in demeanour when dealing with black parents.

Demie and Mclean's report *Narrowing the Achievement Gap of Disadvantaged Pupils* (2017) confirms Shand-Baptiste's (2020) comments, as it indicates that from nursery age (before any formal mental assessment), there is a possibility for a black child to be labelled as a "troublemaker." "Psychological and educational assessments to identify conditions such as attention deficit hyperactive disorder (ADHD), dyslexia, and Asperger's syndrome are often given to white children but are not routinely considered for a black child until after their behaviour involves the law," which basically means when black children are much older and already a product of the self-fulfilling prophesy of the adults in their lives. The report also speaks about "cycles of harm and intergenerational trauma," stating that inequality "begins at birth and follows children into educational settings." We know that anti-racist practice in the early years will also make a massive difference to black children with additional needs who are routinely assessed as having bad behaviour. The same goes for highly intelligent black children who become bored and disinterested in their settings and then "act up" because practitioners are not providing the right kind of challenge for their learning needs.

We have to acknowledge that our best intentions for every child in our setting can be undermined by this kind of implicit bias which leads us to form quick decisions about a situation or a person without necessarily being consciously aware of it. Our brains form biases by using knowledge about social situations, attitudes, cultures, stereotypes, emotional reactions, prior experiences, and our "24/7" exposure to the media. All of this can significantly skew our judgement. Our brains process information in pretty much the same way as our smart phone functions, meaning that what we see is only a tiny part of what is actually going on. In the background there are thousands of different bits of information being processed. What we actually process on a conscious level is only a very small part of the information we receive. Our conscious mind processes 40 to 50 pieces of information per second but our unconscious mind pulls in about 11 million pieces of information per second without us realising that we are taking in this information. The information we process on a subconscious level can sometimes impact how we interact with the children in our care without us being aware of it. Diagrams 4.2 and 4.3 explain and give examples of how these sorts of biases can affect the young children in our care. This is by no means an exhaustive list of unconscious biases but rather an example of some of them and how they may impact on young black children (Diagram 4.2).

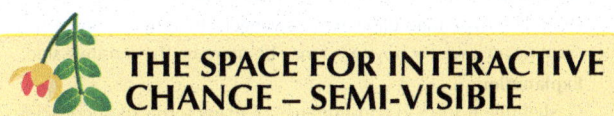

THE SPACE FOR INTERACTIVE CHANGE – SEMI-VISIBLE

Questions for reflection:

1   Think on times in your setting when, on reflection, these types of biases were possible drivers for how practitioners interacted with children.
2. What could your setting put in place to help to manage these situations (Diagram 4.3)?

Diagram 4.2 The impact of unconscious bias on children in the early years.

Affinity bias

Explanation:
This is when you unconsciously relate to people who are similar to you – race, culture, class, or like-mindedness. We all want to be around people we can relate to; the issue is when you unconsciously show preference which can result in clouding your judgement.

Impact:
The impact on pupils is that the pupils you favour are very aware they are favoured and the pupils you don't favour learn that they are not worth your time and attention and are very aware that they are being unfairly treated.

Gender bias

Explanation:
This is when you subconsciously act on deep-seated beliefs you may hold about gender roles and stereotypes. This can become even more complex when race is introduced as a factor. Girls wear pink, boys wear blue, girls play with dolls, boys play with cars. Boys do not dress up and watch *Frozen* and girls do not play football or pretend to be superheroes.

Impact:
We unconsciously associate certain words with different genders. Words that imply leadership, aggression, physicality are coded into our language as masculine and words that convey nurturing, supporting, caring are coded into our language as feminine. We also have to be aware to manage the bias that black girls and black women are always seen as "strong" and not needing the protection or support that white girls and white women need. So little black girls can sometimes be seen as not feminine enough to be princesses or little black boys should be hypermasculine, with "swagger," thereby unconsciously creating an issue for boys who may be more on the sensitive side.

Gaslighting

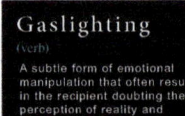

Gaslighting
(verb)
A subtle form of emotional manipulation that often results in the recipient doubting their perception of reality and their sanity.

Explanation:
Gaslighting is the sad consequence of many forms of unconscious bias. It is the act of sowing the seeds of doubt in a targeted individual or group to force them to question their thoughts, their memories, their lived experiences, and events that happen around them.

Impact:
Sadly, children are regularly gaslighted. They are made to doubt their abilities, they are indoctrinated into a sense of inferiority, there is a steady erosion of their self-worth. Discriminatory education will result in children becoming unmotivated, undereducated, and unprepared for further studies in their school lives. Children are also inadvertently gaslighted when the curriculum does not celebrate the identity of all the children who live in this country.

(Continued)

Diagram 4.2 Continued

The horn effect	**Explanation:**

Explanation:
When there is a focus on one particularly negative feature about a child and this clouds the view to all their other qualities.

Impact:
One mistake or flaw does not entirely represent the whole person. Our frustrations with a child can become unconsciously validated when they exhibit an annoying habit that is perceived as stereotypically black. The child may be non-conforming for example, tending to lash out when adults try to interrupt their play or other children try to play with the toys they are playing with. This child may automatically be assessed as having behavioural problems, rather than assessed as having any additional needs. This then sets the stage of blurring the other qualities the child has: for example, ritual play or the fact that they are beginning to play alongside other children for short periods of time or that they love animals and always wants to talk about their dog, thereby creating missed opportunities to engage positively in their learning.

Diagram 4.3 Microaggressions in the early years.

Microaggressions

Microaggressions are the everyday, thinly veiled instances of subtle and direct bias towards groups that are protected under the *Equality Act 2010*. The difference between microaggressions and overt discrimination is that people who commit microaggressions might not even be aware that they are doing it.

Examples of microaggressions in the early years

Stereotyping children on their race, social status, backgrounds

High/low expectations of children based on personal bias

Combing children's hair, changing their clothes because of the educator's personal preference – "Why do they dress her like a boy?"

Feeding children food that they are not allowed for religious reasons because you personally do not see anything wrong with it.

Assuming children are too young to understand when they are being treated differently.

Assuming that certain children cannot have certain experiences based on preconceived notions of who they are.

Lying to cover yourself if a child reports something negative about an adult in their learning environment – leading them to doubt their own reality.

Disbelieving/believing children based on preconceived ideas about their race, social status, and backgrounds.

THE SPACE FOR TRANSFORMATIVE CHANGE – INVISIBLE

Questions for reflection:

1. In regard to the grid above, can you discuss situations when microaggressions have happened in your setting?
2. How will a better understanding about microaggressions help to shape your future interactions with young children?

None of us are one-dimensional human beings: the hearts and minds journey towards anti-racist practice

Most of us would never describe ourselves as racist. In fact, we may even think of ourselves as liberal and open-minded individuals; however, our implicit attitudes can often be at odds with our consciously held beliefs. There are many opinions being expressed about whether unconscious-bias training actually works. Personally, I believe that it is possible to address our biases if we become aware of them; but becoming aware of our unconscious biases empowers us to manage them only if training is part of an explicit ongoing process that drives anti-racist practice. We shouldn't expect to do one-off unconscious bias training and then imagine that somehow this will be the magic pill that can change people into adopting anti-racist practice. Anti-racist practice is not just about what you do; it is about who you are. To be perfectly honest, I am not sure how I feel about training that assumes that there is something to fix in some people and not in others. There is a fine line to tread here, especially if people feel targeted. I am far more in favour of ongoing team building which is embedded into the function of the organisation. In my opinion, we can achieve far more by building our capacity to cultivate empathy.

All of us are imperfect, complex, multi-faceted human beings and when we interact with other human beings, we have to practice remembering our own humanity to help us to not "other" people who operate outside of our comfort zone. We do not have to like everyone, but we can practice shaping within ourselves how we perceive others, so we become conditioned to feel and respond with empathy, respect, and kindness. This is a process of training our minds to intentionally process information alongside training our hearts to intentionally process emotions. When we humanise people who are different to us, we immediately focus on the person and not on their perceived difference, and we can treat them in the way we ourselves want to be treated. We can start to acknowledge that if a criminal, black or white, attacks us or burgles our house then that criminal behaviour belongs to that individual and is not attributable to their race. If you are attacked or targeted because of your race, then that is different; it is explicit racial discrimination on the part of the attacker.

Dr Ibram Kendi argues that to be anti-racist is to actively think that there is no right or wrong behaviour nor is there any inferiority or superiority in regard to racial groups. He states that anti-racists have a deep understanding that individuals behaving well or badly is, purely and simply, individuals behaving well or badly. Their behaviour should never be perceived as being representative of their race (Kendi, 2019). When we stereotype someone or interact with them according to stereotypical expectations of their race, we set off a reinforcement loop that actually helps to create and perpetuate unproductive behaviours and tensions which can feel cold, unwelcoming, or otherwise insincere to the other person. It then becomes very easy to fall into the trap of "they always" or "they never"; what if we could erase what we think we know from our interactions and intentionally have an open mind and an open heart in our interactions with others? What if we assume the best and notice each interaction for what it is so that we can begin to chip away at negative stereotyping?

The process of working with hearts and minds also involves creating a healthy emotional distance from which to process rationally even while empathising. If we start to over-empathise and become overtaken by emotions, we can create an energy field that deflects from the issue and focuses on the individual exhibiting the emotion in an unhealthy way. Look at it this way: I come into your office and tell you that my dad has died and I am understandably a bit emotional but you over-empathise to the point where you are crying more than I am, even though we are not close friends and you have never met my dad. So now I am finding it difficult to get to my original intent for coming into your office in the first place, which was to tell you that I won't be able to attend that important client meeting as I need some time to travel home to make arrangements for my dad's funeral. Sometimes we need to challenge ourselves about whether our emotions are more about us than they are a healthy dose of empathy for another person's situation, or if we are using excessive emotion as an unconscious strategy to divert attention away from our actions and create focus instead on how bad the other person is making us feel. I have seen this happen time and time again and, to my frustration, all it does is protect and generate sympathy for the offender and leaves the offence undealt with.

Healthy anti-racist practice also does not involve over-internalising the predicament of others to the point where we gaslight ourselves into believing that everything is our fault. If we become emotionally activated by another person's experience, then this may be about feeling a bit uncomfortable about uncovering an unconscious bias which is more than likely due to our social conditioning. This is never about harsh self-condemnation but about setting ourselves free to own our practice and work on what needs to be changed. The journey towards anti-racist practice has to be an intentional choice for action at some point. It is possible for us to become more aware but still choose to sit on the outskirts of the issue, for various reasons; I imagine that this would only add to our internal struggles, because it then becomes more difficult to unsee what our eyes have been opened to and unknow what our minds have learned. I like to think of human beings as living the story of their lives but there is a difference between being the author of that story and just being a character. Thinking in this way allows our reality to shift away from being resigned to "it is what it is" and "I am doing my best considering" to designing "who I want to be" and "how I will make a difference for humanity?"

"Stop for a minute … now think about it": the power of cognitive reappraisal

Mann and Ferguson (2015) found that negative implicit bias about other people can be unlearned with positive information and enough reasoning. I can't tell anyone *what* to think but, surely, we can figure out *how* to think if we care to challenge ourselves on our deep-seated stereotypical perceptions. The big questions regarding our belief systems should be: How justified are my perceptions? If I deconstruct these perceptions, do they make sense? We can then help ourselves to develop a coherent belief system by:

- Understanding that our perceptions are based on incomplete and imperfect information.
- Checking a variety of sources that either confirm, refute, or challenge our beliefs.
- Testing whether our beliefs make a logically strong argument in the face of research and deeper thinking.

I know this feels like a lot of time and effort, but once we are in the practice of deconstructing our thinking it usually becomes second nature and does not feel as time-consuming as when we just started doing it. I have chosen to do a profile on Jamaicans in regard to the grid in Diagram 4.1. The information in the profile is backed up by first-hand experience but I also ensured that the variety of sources to challenge our thinking is freely available on official sites on the internet with very little effort required to seek it out. Despite my knowledge of the country I was born in, I was petrified to take my husband home for our delayed honeymoon (there is a whole story, but that is for another time) and to introduce him to my family. I had visions of us dodging bullets, being kidnapped before we even laid eyes on my family, or of being held at gunpoint and robbed of all our belongings. Such is the power of the media; it was able to distort the views of a native Jamaican returning to her place of birth. It took my sisters asking me what was wrong with me to snap me back to the reality that we faced no more danger going to Jamaica, a popular tourist destination, than we faced going to Spain. Let us indulge in a little perception *vs.* research and deeper thinking exercise – cognitive reappraisal, so to speak.

Perception: Jamaica is a poor country. People who come to Britain from Jamaica are looking for a better life and are likely to be illegal migrants living off the welfare system.

Research and deeper thinking: Even the wealthiest first world countries have a number of citizens who live in poverty and even the poorest of nations have a number of people who live in extreme wealth. Britain is no different and, although small, Jamaica is no different either. Jamaica is described as a poor "third world" country but this little island is rich in natural resources and has a climate that is ideal for agriculture and tourism. Despite being a poorer country, Jamaica is classed as an upper-middle-income country by the World Bank. Jamaican people are no longer answering to the call of the "Motherland" to come and rebuild, and, therefore, it needs to be acknowledged that people travel to the UK for a number of reasons – study, business, holidays, visiting families, funerals and weddings etc. and, of course, people who are trying to make a better life for themselves and their loved ones do come to live in the UK. This situation is not peculiar to Jamaicans. Nor is this situation considered strange for the number of UK citizens who move to live all over the world for the expressed intention of seeking a better life for themselves and their loved ones.

I was unable to find any statistics about Jamaicans who are classed as illegal migrants but, anecdotally, we know they exist. While everyone is focused on the number of people who come to live in the UK, very little is known about the numbers who leave. Between 2010 and 2019, the Migration Observatory reports that approximately 37,000 people without leave to remain in the UK, leave the country on a yearly basis; and during the same time period, voluntary returns have outnumbered enforced returns. Also, it should be noted that illegal migrants have no recourse to public funds. They may work illegally but there is a market in the UK that is willing and able to exploit this for private gain.

Perception: Jamaican people are uncivilised and they live in squalid conditions.

Research and deeper thinking: What if it were my perception that British people love their dogs more than they love their own children? That would be a sweeping generalisation that would be quite offensive, as is the perception above. It should be just as obvious that generalised perceptions like this are based in accepting what has been heard without bothering to check for validity. Furthermore, poor does not mean squalid. Without question, there are many, many people who are mired in poverty and have to struggle to look after their families and, like anywhere else in the world, Jamaica has its own tiered system based on money, class, and education but underneath it all the notion of respectability is huge for Jamaican people. Being vulgar, idle, rude, drunk, or obscene is seen as unacceptable or, as we call it in Jamaica, "raw-chaw" behaviour. This "raw-chaw" behaviour is what we have become used to seeing from tourists visiting the island. We hold respectability very highly and most people aim to be highly respectable, no matter their background.

There is a subset of our culture that is based in overt sexuality (dancehall, for example) but dancehall is not the lifestyle of all Jamaicans and I do not apologise for the Jamaicans whose lifestyle this is – especially as it has its roots in slavery, where black people were sexually fetishised, and some people choose to reclaim and enjoy that experience for themselves. Furthermore, apologising for dancehall would be like a British person apologising for punk rockers or the well-publicised overt sexual behaviour that occurs at a Glastonbury festival between strangers. In many ways, a subculture has developed in the UK where second and subsequent generations of Jamaicans have been displaced and have developed their own "Jamaican" identity as a way of belonging in a country that does not accept them as British even when they are born here.

Perception: Jamaicans have dysfunctional family lives. The women all have children with a lot of different men.

Research and deeper thinking: Women all over the world have different children with different men for various reasons best known to them. I don't see it as my responsibility to defend or dispute this fact. In the Jamaican context, and especially amongst the poorest in society, the legacy of slavery has a lot to do with this issue: family units were a fluid concept for black people during slavery. Slaves were seen as property, not people, so separating families was a usual occurrence, as was indiscriminate breeding to produce more slaves for the Empire. Marriage is still seen as a middle-class institution in Jamaica and therefore is generally perceived as being for those who are better off in society, who can afford to be married. Poorer Jamaicans generally live in "common-law" marriages or consensual unions. Legal marriages, when they do happen amongst poorer Jamaicans, generally tend to occur later in the relationship, after children are born and after the couple has attained some degree of economic security. Consensual unions are rife in Britain across racial and cultural groups but appear to be considered distasteful when associated with black families. On a personal level, it would have been outrageous for me to consider living with someone or having a baby before marriage. That would have been a family scandal that would have reverberated around the world!

Family life is central to Jamaicans, even when it is not within a conventional marriage union. Amongst poorer Jamaicans, it is not uncommon for three generations to share a home. Grandmothers look after the children, women work so they can feed their children, and, despite popular opinion, non-residential fathers are not automatically absentee fathers. Fathers usually contribute – I agree sometimes sporadically – to supporting their children. Most families share a main meal together on weekday evenings and everybody and their neighbour partakes of the traditional Saturday soup. Sunday has its own tradition; everyone has a large family lunch, even poorer families. This includes chicken, fish, or, in my family, pot-roasted beef, rice and peas, Irish potatoes and vegetables, with a side of the most amazing avocado pears picked from the trees on our property.

If the media is to be believed, in contemporary Britain, black afro-Caribbean children all have single mothers, absentee fathers who are in jail, no family structure, and dysfunctional family lives. We know this is not the case but if it were, this would be a phenomenon that is peculiar to Britain. Why would this be so prevalent here in the UK? This needs to be looked into far more deeply, past very glib stereotypical labelling. One reason, to explore further, is the criminal justice system's propensity for arbitrarily sending black people to jail for minor offences and the use of prisoners as cheap and forced labour (another legacy of slavery) to generate profit for prisons and private companies. Just something to think about in this vicious cycle of labelling and stereotyping.

Perception: Jamaica is riddled with crime and is a very dangerous place, therefore Jamaican people are dangerous.

Research and deeper thinking: We do have serious issues with crime in Jamaica for a number of reasons, especially with the deportation of sophisticated and ruthless criminals who have honed their skills in other countries. Jamaica is small but it should be noted that, as with any other country, the causes of crime are very much the same as anywhere else in the world: unemployment, poverty, the justice system – these issues are related and interconnected. Crime reporting regarding Jamaica is often sensationalised in mass media as if crimes of a similar nature do not happen across the globe. However, the majority of crime in Jamaica is concentrated in the inner-city areas and, for the most part, the rest of Jamaica is relatively safe, experiencing little or no crime over sustained periods of time. We have a Maroon Village in Jamaica called Accompong that has not recorded a single murder in over 250 years! So yes, we have serious issues in a few hotspot areas, and we all know that wherever there are opportunities to make money, there are people who are ready to exploit those opportunities; but to tar all Jamaicans with the criminal brush is again that broad, stereotypical assumption that disregards the past, present, and future accomplishments of a whole population of people, who for the most part live normal, uneventful lives.

In the UK as in Jamaica, there is a lot of work to be done with regard to the poorest people in society becoming frustrated at "busting their guts" for low wages and no chance of having anything extra to enjoy in their lives. Sadly, there are much quicker ways to make money and live a life that is otherwise unavailable to poorer people. In the UK, second and subsequent generations of Jamaicans are treated with suspicion, routinely labelled, even though they are generally innocent, treated poorly in the education system, criminalised, traumatised by unfair stop and searches, and much more; unfortunately, this is normal, everyday life for these youngsters who have to fight through the system to stay out of jail and become successful citizens. It seems fairly obvious to me that these young people could very easily be drawn into an easier way of doing things in a society that is hostile towards them and has, in general, already written them off as criminals and "good for nothing."

Throughout our lives we subsume a myriad of values, ideas, ideals, and beliefs. However, we tend not to challenge the longest-standing of these because our core beliefs become integrated into our identity from sources that we trust a lot and question very little. As we get older and seek knowledge of our own volition, often without the process of unlearning, new knowledge then becomes layered on top of these deeply held core beliefs. In an effort to maintain a sense of selfhood we compartmentalise knowledge to ensure that it does not interfere with our sense of self.

So, that being said, if we hold the futures of children in our hands, as educators, do we not have a duty to challenge our long-standing beliefs to ensure that the children in our care experience a fair education system that is not marred by the filters that have been installed in our minds through our own personal, subjective experiences? This challenge cannot be delegated or outsourced. It is a personal journey and, at times, must be a collective journey, for educators if we truly want to make a difference in the lives of our pupils.

A better way

If we learned how to converse with each other in a natural way about our differences and our similarities, this journey towards a more equitable society would be a much easier one. What if we opened conversations with questions like those in Diagram 4.4?

Conversation is a great way to get to know someone else and to discover that we are really not that different after all. Allow me to tell you of my own personal example of stereotypical perception. The Jamaican tradition of Saturday soup is alive and well with me. We have many versions of Saturday soup; red peas soup, fish soup, mannish water, and so on and so forth. The difference is usually in the meat or peas/beans and chosen vegetables used in making the soup. Jamaican chicken soup is one of my favourite things to eat – a burst of flavours and totally awesome in my opinion. The soup is made with chicken, nutritional vegetables – carrots, pumpkin, chayote or "cho-cho" as we call it back home in Jamaica; it also has potatoes, dumplings, yam, and amazing herbs and seasonings (I went a bit heavy on the thyme for this soup) including scotch bonnet peppers for that extra kick.

My Saturday soup looks like the bowl full of goodness in Figure 4.1!

Guess what? My two boys hate Jamaican soup with a passion! If it's soup, it needs to be cream of something for them! My older son cannot understand why his food has to float around in a vat of liquid, and my younger son wants to know why he has to chase his chicken around the

Diagram 4.4 The "better-way" conversation grid.

Do you live with your grandparents? What is that like?	Describe a family tradition?	What is the most important thing about your culture?	Are you a religious person? Tell me about your religion and why it is important to you?
Describe a cultural/ family dish? How is it made?	What is your favourite book/ movie?	What holidays do you celebrate?	What is your favourite meal? How is it made?
How do you feel if people are unkind to you because of the colour of your skin?	Can we be friends? What do you like to do?	What do you watch on TV?	What do you want to be when you grow up? Why?

Figure 4.1 Saturday soup.

bowl (I despair!). According to them, Jamaican soup defies the concept of what soup is supposed to be; how rude! I have to admit to being a bit hurt and wondering where I went wrong with them because I make amazing Jamaican soup! I presumed that love of all kinds of Jamaican food would be automatic with my sons because of their heritage but I quickly learned that in this respect, I had my own version of stereotypical perception.

As British families, we are not that different. A national poll done in 2020 found that British parents' top concerns for their children centred around overuse of social media, overexposure to screen time, internet safety, unhealthy eating, lack of physical activity, depression, and suicide. Despite black families having to factor the effects of systemic racism into their equation, there is far more that unites us than divides us as British families. All of us may have dominant perspectives but, by being open to the views of others, we can train ourselves to see the perspectives of others.

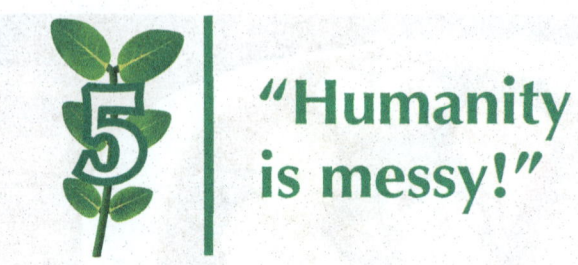

"Humanity is messy!"

We are at a place in the journey where we need to check in with all the passengers and make sure everybody is ok and that no one is too uncomfortable. When the car is full, there is always somebody that has to sit on that hard hump in the middle of the back seat. We need to imagine what it feels like for that person so that we can make some adjustments and maybe make a few extra stops to give them some relief. The journey can be far more difficult for some people than it is for others because for some people, if they lose their beliefs then nothing makes sense, which can create panic as they then feel in danger of losing themselves. If we oversimplify the process of change without being mindful of the people who will find it most challenging then we are in danger of creating a situation where we send someone into crisis mode, which makes them dig their heels in, even when faced with overwhelming evidence. Imagine trying to come to terms with feeling as if the way you live your life has been built on lies! I believe, as a purely human reaction, everything inside of you will seek alternative facts to make it all make sense. As practitioners, we know that children learn at different rates and in different ways and adults are just the same. To successfully get through this journey towards anti-racist practice in our settings we have to invest time and create space within our practice for people to learn at their own pace, while putting in the support that aids positive change.

Different perspectives

As a black woman, my instinctive feeling is that people must know what to do to make things "right"; after all, it is simply about basic respect and

DOI: 10.4324/9781003247807-5

human kindness. However, writing this book has helped me to realise that the whole social phenomenon of racism cannot hinge on what is "right" and "wrong," as these concepts are subjective and set in the standards and customs of our own cultures. We are all products of the society we live in, our backgrounds, our experiences, our beliefs, and our values. The notions of "right" and "wrong" are not so clear when you think of the issue of racial division in this way. Therefore, we have to accept that there will never be a nice, neat narrative when it comes to racism. As a person who works tirelessly for human rights and equitable education, with early years being my passion, I readily assume a standpoint that expects that everyone has at least a basic understanding of the historical legacies of slavery and that persistent inequality in contemporary Britain is ethically wrong. However, this way of thinking is actually a little bit "holier than thou" and assumes that anyone who does not agree with my perspective is somehow lacking in "morals." This way of thinking oversimplifies the issue of racism by viewing white communities through the lens of "good white people" and "bad white people," with the good white people being the ones who have "taken a knee," so to speak, and publicly spoken out against racism. Racism is not a moral choice; however, as early years practitioners, we need to employ moral intent, with sincerity, respect, and professional love, to implement anti-racist practice as an aspect of our core beliefs.

We work with the concept of "moral development" in the early years. Though we may not highlight it explicitly in our everyday practice, it is present in the ways we help children to develop standards of "right" and "wrong" based on social and cultural norms. Aspects of this process sit beneath the legal umbrella of "British values." Within our practice, we are all legally tasked with the responsibility to embed democracy, the rule of law, individual liberty, mutual respect, and tolerance of those of different faiths and beliefs. If Britain prides itself on these values, why does life generally feel so unfair for ethnic minority people and their children? It is interesting to me that Piaget, in his work on moral development, was not really interested in whether children broke the rules, but more in the moral reasoning of children. He had sets of questions to probe children's understanding of rules, moral responsibility, and justice. I will try to frame these questions for younger children, but this is a great exercise for us adults as well (Diagram 5.1).

Diagram 5.1 Adapted from Piaget's moral reasoning (1971).

Children's understanding of rules leads to questions like these:
- Who makes up the rules of what is "wrong" and what is "right"?
- Why did they make up the rules?
- Do you think we can change these rules?

Children's understanding of moral responsibility leads to questions like these:
- When "bad" things happen, whose fault is it?
- Is the behaviour "bad" because it is "bad," or because it made somebody cry?
- Is there a difference between your friend who was not paying attention and broke your favourite toy by accident and the boy/girl who is not your friend who broke your favourite toy on purpose?

Children's understanding of justice leads to questions like these:
- If your friend broke your favourite toy by accident, should they be punished?
- If the boy/girl who is not your friend broke your toy by accident, should they be punished?
- The toy is broken, whether it was done by accident or on purpose. Should the punishment be the same?
- When someone does something wrong, are they always punished?

Through this level of deconstruction and decentring, children learn that people make rules and people can change rules if they want to. This process also begins to help children to understand subjective facts and internal responsibility. Morality is one of the reasons that human beings are so unique. Human beings have a shared, broad consensus about what is wrong and what is right when it comes to human behaviour. However, we can't forget the concepts of subjective facts and internal responsibility. If we apply a moralistic approach to racism without due regard to subjective facts and internal responsibility, all this will allow for is the positioning of people in nice, neat categories of "wrong" and "right."

I do not believe this positioning is particularly helpful in shifting conscious or unconscious bias that may be present when working with young children. As a society, even when we have a basic agreement to live by a set of universal rules that guide our social behaviour, we should not forget to factor in the much wider spectrum of moral values. You only have to walk into any nursery environment at pick-up and drop-off times to see this phenomenon fully displayed between parents and children and also in the interactions between the community and staff who hail from all kinds of different social and/or cultural backgrounds. All of these dynamics come to rest, especially in "inner-city" areas, in a multicultural society with a legacy of slavery and where human beings from all walks of life co-exist with each other. Humanity is messy; therefore, racism and, by association, anti-racism are also messy. I feel sure that if we don't engage the hearts and minds of people, as we spoke about in Chapter 4, then we are all destined to stay in this very deep, dark, dank, smelly pit called racism. Racism connects with the lives of *all* human beings in any multicultural society in different forms and on different levels and even when they live in predominantly white areas.

"I am not racist, but ..."

This statement is a result of not only how extensively and deeply racial ideals are embedded in systems, written and unwritten policies, and in the law, but also how entrenched it is in the practices and beliefs that reproduce, excuse, and perpetuate widespread prejudicial treatment of ethnic minority people. Do you recall ever hearing any of the statements from Diagram 5.2 being said to or about black children throughout your professional lives? I have heard various versions of these sentiments.

Diagram 5.2 Logical racism.

Said to children "..." **(Said about children)**

"Not you again!" **(Well of course it is! These children always behave badly.)**

"I do hope we aren't going to have another day like yesterday!" **(Not that I really expect any better.)**

"You are just like your brother/sister." **(Well! What do you expect from that family?)**

(The majority of the children are black, so behaviour is a problem here.)

"Here, let me help you." **(I know this is hard for him, it is not his fault that he is as thick as two short planks, bless his heart.)**

(This child is from a nice family. I'll just clear up this little misunderstanding with his/her mum.)

"Stealing is not nice!" **(This child is poor, and his/her dad must be a criminal so he/she must be the one stealing from the lunch boxes, it's just natural behaviour to them, isn't it?)**

"Well, what did you do for him/her to hit you?" **(Black children are naturally aggressive. I am sure the little so-and-so did something first.)**

"Logical racism" is absorbed into our minds through a process similar to diffusion: we breathe it in because it is present in the atmosphere around us. Carmel and Hamilton (1967), who coined the term "institutional racism," explain the difference between individual acts of racism and institutional racism. Institutional racism operates as "established and respected forces in the society, and thus receives far less public condemnation than [individual racism]" (p. 4). They also explain that

> institutional racism relies on the active and pervasive operation of anti-black attitudes and practices. A sense of superior group position prevails: whites are 'better' than blacks; therefore, blacks should be subordinated to whites. This is a racist attitude and it permeates the society, on both the individual and institutional level.
>
> (p. 5)

Racism is so complex that even some victims of systemic racism may hold and perpetuate a racist perspective against their own race. There is nothing more powerful as a defence against accused racism than to point out that "so and so" – e.g., Kemi Badendoch (UK member of Parliament and Secretary of State for International Trade at the time of writing), who is black, or Priti Patel (UK MP and previously Secretary of State for the Home Department), who is Asian – agrees with the party standpoint so it couldn't possibly be racist. As we say in Jamaica, "argument dun!," trite and reductive though the position may be.

THE SPACE FOR TRANSFORMATIVE CHANGE – INVISIBLE

Questions for reflection:

1. "I am not anti-black, but I do believe that white people are better than black people at most things." Discuss why someone might think this is true? How might this belief impact on practice in the early years?
2. Discuss how this belief might be supported by institutional racism

Sore points

Any discussions around racism are understandably highly emotive and triggering in many ways for all involved especially as there is still a high level of ignorance (sometimes intentional) surrounding conversations regarding race. Have you ever heard the unfiltered version of what someone of another race truly thinks about you? I have, from a colleague whom I thought of as a close friend, and the underlying vitriol was shocking. After having a conversation late one evening, my phone somehow managed to tape a conversation my friend was having with her husband around their dinner table. And before you ask, I have never told her, nor have I acted differently towards her. I learned to value this experience as a gift and to question more deeply why someone who has openly professed to be non-racist, would speak so differently within the privacy of her own home.

Whilst there are certain issues I hold a firm standpoint on, equality being one of them, I had to stop and wonder what someone might hear me saying around my dinner table if I was comfortable in my assumption that my conversation was totally private. I understand far more now than I did then because I know far more now about systemic racism than I did then. What do we know about systemic racism? We know that it stems from slavery, and we know that this is also a very sore point as many people think it is ridiculous that an "event" that happened hundreds of years ago should even be considered relevant in our lives today. An "event" that continued for hundreds of years ceases to be an event and must be acknowledged as a way of life that also helped to set the stage for mainstream British societal and cultural traditions.

Allow me to ask a couple of uncomfortable questions of my white colleagues; do you, somewhere in the depths of your being, feel that you are better than black people? And if and when you allow yourself to think about it, are you even a tiny bit thankful that you are not black? If in all honesty you do, then we have to admit that the effects of white superiority have lasted for the same hundreds of years as the effects of slavery, so slavery is as relevant today as it has ever been. By now I think my readers realise that I think in graphics and find it easier to communicate my thoughts in this way. I can't help associating racism with a tree, in part because of the prominence of trees in photos and depictions of the lynching and beating of slaves, but also in terms of the concept of "the tree of good and evil" and what makes this social phenomenon grow and thrive (Diagram 5.3).

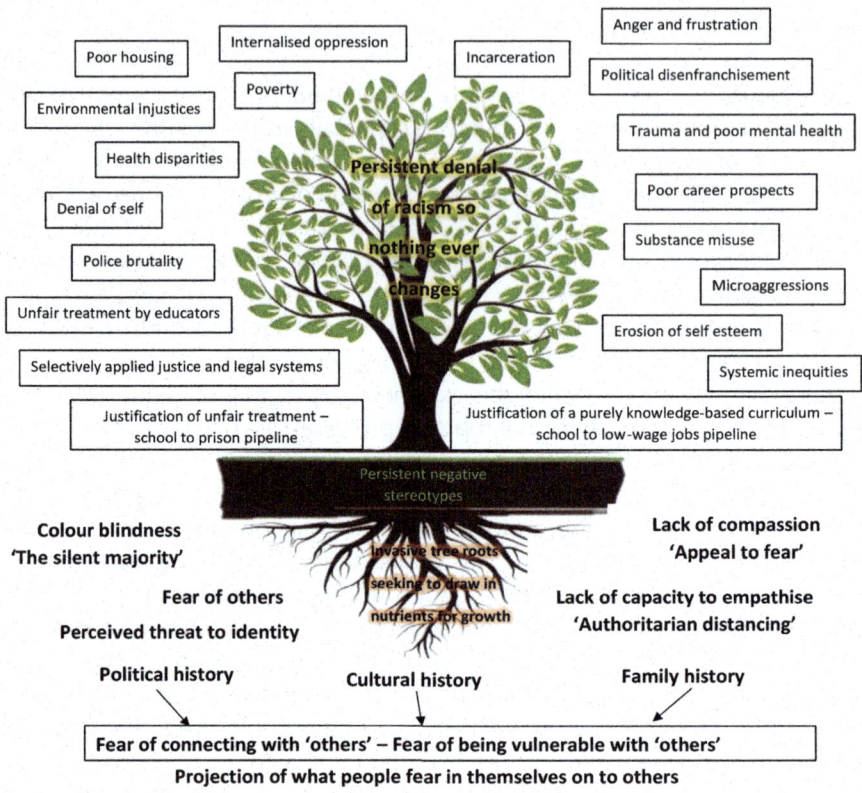

Diagram 5.3 The racism tree.

Diagram 5.3 is overwhelmingly negative as it depicts the effects of racism as multi-factorial, multi-levelled, and traumatic in various ways and to various degrees for people who experience racism as part of their daily life. There is honestly no upside to experiencing racism as a central factor in a person's life so there is not really a more palatable way to share this information. Seeing it all together in the diagram is quite harsh and may even feel slightly fantastic to some, but let us dig beneath this racism tree to see if it is real and to discover what keeps this tree alive and well.

THE SPACE FOR TRANSFORMATIVE CHANGE – INVISIBLE

Questions for reflection:

1. In regard to the racism tree, can you unpick and discuss how the experiences of the black child from their earliest involvement in their learning environments could impact on how they perceive themselves?
2. What is the difference for children who are treated in the ways that all children should be treated in early education?
3. How will the knowledge garnered from the racism tree support any changes to the practice in your setting?

The racism tree depicts the sad reality of how a lack of capacity to empathise and feel compassion for people who are of a different race continues to perpetuate poor outcomes for black and ethnic minority children and adults.

THE SPACE FOR TRANSFORMATIVE CHANGE – INVISIBLE

Group exercise:

1. Design an "anti-racism" tree. What would feed this tree from the roots? And how would the branches and leaves support positive change for social ecology?

A lot of people reading this book are perhaps thinking "This is really heavy," and were probably expecting a "pick up and go" best-practice guide to implementing anti-racist practice in early years settings. I wish I could provide this because that would mean that we have cracked it; that we have discovered a tried and tested approach that will have the outcome of "best" end results. The thing is, racism is heavy for the people who live with it on a daily basis and trying to explain it without sharing the weight of the problem would, in essence, be making light of its severity and the profound impact it has on people's lives. Unpacking racism is a process that will take us out of our comfort zones if we are truly trying to learn and make a difference. In the early years we talk about "process rather than just outcome" which, when working with young children, means that we focus less on the outcome of every child in the class producing a painting to be displayed on the walls and focus more on the processes and techniques involved in how children learn best. Best outcomes are a journey, not a destination and they require us to be present in the moment, not projecting past the step-by-step process because we are hyper-focused on the reward. Don't get me wrong, the reward is important, but predicating success on an overall end result may lead to frustration and disappointment. If we are in the moment and working through the process, we will achieve far more success with the little steps along the way.

I love the early years! The more I look at the pedagogy and practices involved, the more I see potential for strategies for real-world change. In the early years, we also work with the concept of "in-the-moment planning" which is a pedagogical approach that involves working with children's interests and supporting their learning by planning in the moment instead of planning in advance. In-the-moment planning requires us to know our statutory duties, understand what needs to be taught, and manoeuvre the curriculum into how children learn. This does not mean that there is no use for advanced planning; we just know that nothing planned is set in stone and we also give due regard to planning that creates opportunities to respond in the moment. While we may plan to address racism in our settings, we have no idea of the various ways in which racism will be manifested. There is real skill involved in being proficient and informed enough to respond in the moment, in what is referred to as "the teachable moment" in in-the-moment planning.

A racially inclusive environment in the early years is a never-ending pursuit that continually places the rights of the child at the centre of the development of anti-racist practice. Alongside embedding the rights of the child, we have to actively explore the perspectives of key workers in our settings in a way that feels safe and inclusive. This all then needs to be tied together within the ethos, environment, pedagogy, philosophy, policies, and practices in the setting that clearly indicate the setting's remit of anti-racist practice to all interested parties. We also have to understand that all of the above is being executed under external societal pressure that, in my experience, generally wants to give the appearance of change while not really changing at all. Our settings are not static: staff come and go; we have times of plenty and times of scarcity (although scarcity is outliving its time at the moment in my opinion! Time for it to move on now); we are constantly tasked with implementing the legal policy remits of changing governments; without the anchors of leadership, motivation, and consistency in our settings, anti-racist practice will be fleeting.

"The lights are on but nobody's home!"

True anti-racist practice can't be internally compartmentalised. This is a bit like turning on the front lights in an unoccupied house in the hopes of deterring burglars, while the rest of the house is in complete darkness. All it would take is a little bit of observation in preparation for the planned robbery to reveal that the lights are on day and night, or else are programmed to come on at a specific time and that there is no normal family activity. Those of us who have watched the movie *Home Alone* have seen what is involved in trying to deter burglars. The same applies to anti-racist practice: something will always expose what we are trying to hide. Disingenuous anti-racist practice can present as performative and a bit like staging the house purely for appearances. There is also a bit of distinction between being non-racist and being anti-racist that applies to this analogy. Anderson (2020) explains that while a non-racist person "does not believe the things a racist believes, non-racist people, do very little to positively change the negative race situation in their personal environment or in this country" (p. 46). So, in this sense, it is a bit like sewing an authentic designer-brand logo onto a lookalike version of the original designer dress. The logo is authentic and while the dress looks pretty, it doesn't feel quite right to wear it, so it remains in the closet on a hanger, doing nothing. Being non-racist is a start but being anti-racist is what makes the difference for the children in our care.

What it feels like to be black in Britain

I am going to attempt to capture the collective experiences of what it feels like to be black in Britain for most black people, first from the experience of the child and then from the experience of the adult.

CASE STUDY 3: THE COLLECTIVE EXPERIENCE OF THE BLACK CHILD IN BRITAIN

The child reports that their teachers do not like them, and they get in trouble a lot, sometimes with no understanding of why this happens. The "other" children in their setting delight in developing new and inventive ways to bully the child, usually because of their kinky hair or the way they speak, and even the teachers laugh and tell the child "don't be so sensitive, it's just a joke"; so nothing is done about the pain and embarrassment the child feels. However, when the child behaves badly (and they will, because they are children), and even sometimes when the child is just standing up for themselves, they are harshly punished without fail. It appears that the joke only applies when you are black. The child learns that they do not have to do very much to get in trouble. The child's personality and self-esteem start to fade away as the system that is supposed to nurture them betrays them instead. The child learns to accept that their teachers generally do not expect much of them.

The child learns that who they are, their needs and their aspirations, are not important. The child learns from when they are very young that their youthful energy and foolish mistakes will not be treated in the same way as their white friends who appear to be given chances to learn from their mistakes. Their white friends appear to expect that, as children, they will be (and should be) protected by the system. The child interacts daily with people they cannot quite trust to have their best interests at heart.

Imagine being a black child in Britain.

THE SPACE FOR TRANSFORMATIVE CHANGE – INVISIBLE

Group exercise:

1. What are some of the ways we, as early years practitioners, can tune into the experiences of the black child so that we are able to start making positive changes to this cycle of harm?

As early years practitioners, we are keenly aware of the importance of parents' involvement in their children's education. Research tells us that when parents are respected as children's first educators and as co-educators, children enjoy learning, have greater self-esteem, behave better, and are far more confident in themselves and their abilities. If parents themselves have survived this cycle of harm with varying degrees of long-term psychological damage, it is entirely feasible that they may feel undervalued, unprepared, and incapable of being involved in their children's learning journeys. Let us look into the experiences of the black adult and how their experiences may hinder their involvement in their children's education and how this might also impact on the messages black parents consciously and unconsciously pass on to their children, thereby adding to the cycle of harm they want to protect their children from.

CASE STUDY 4: THE COLLECTIVE EXPERIENCE OF THE BLACK ADULT IN BRITAIN

Imagine living your life always operating with a perceived elevated threat level because of the colour of your skin. You are always on edge because the system is unfairly stacked against you and the possibility that there is intent for harm is an everyday prospect. You are always worried about your own safety and the safety of your children. You are regularly told to "go home" or "go back to where you come from," but this is home and this is where you come from; you were born here in Britain, your parents were born here, and your parents' parents were born here. You go overboard in disciplining your children in an attempt to keep them on the "straight and narrow." You try to teach your children the value of education but from very early on they begin to be aware of how unfair the world is. You live with stress concerning your children as the staff in the educational setting seem to enjoy letting you know how "bad" your child is and what a poor job you do as a parent; not that they expected much from you anyway, as they assume that you fit all of the negative black stereotypes. Again, you discipline your child, for the fear of them being labelled but also to teach them to walk that very thin tightrope to stay out of trouble.

Now you fear social services' involvement as well. The staff keep telling you that your child has additional needs even though you know that he is just bored in nursery; in the meanwhile, your friend who has got a child with additional needs is struggling to get proper support for her child.

Your worries are bigger than your child's learning environment as you are not sure how you can ever be a role model for your child when the media constantly tells you, and everyone else, how bad you are. You learn practical things, such as not to carry books into a book store or not to walk into a clothing store with shopping bags, and you try to teach "black" survival tips to your children from when they are very young. As a black person, you learn that it is your job to bend yourself out of shape to make sure white people are comfortable around you. You learn to make eye contact and smile in an attempt to reassure people that you are harmless, but your children are too young to really understand this stuff, nor should they have to! You are labelled as genetically lazy and work-shy for struggling to be employed in a system that discriminates against you and, for some of your friends and family, the toxic trio of domestic abuse, mental ill-health, and substance misuse is a prevalent factor in their lives. You internalise the idea that you have to work harder than everyone else to get anywhere, and if you manage to fight through the system to get your qualifications in a professional field, you are treated with suspicion or anger and people hold an uneasy feeling about you because they assume that the colour of your skin somehow means that you have intent for fraud. Even when you work hard for what you have, people assume that you must have acquired it through criminal activity. You learn to take it on the chin when you are treated poorly in nice restaurants and five-star hotels and your white friends don't seem to ever notice how poorly you are being treated, so you learn that no amount of assimilation can shield you from racism. To top it all off you are viewed as having a chip on your shoulder or accused of having a poor attitude if you question any of this.

Imagine being a black adult in Britain.

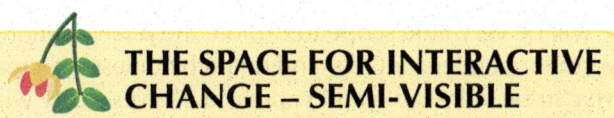

THE SPACE FOR INTERACTIVE CHANGE – SEMI-VISIBLE

Questions for reflection:

1. How will knowing what it feels like to be a black adult in Britain shape the conversations staff in your settings have with parents?
2. What could your setting put in place to value parents as their children's first educators, and encourage parents to be actively involved in their child's education?

To support these discussions, let us unpack the racism tree a bit more. Racism is fed by a *fear of others*; society regularly reinforces the "goodness" of white people and the "badness" of black people, and this is easily absorbed in a subliminal way into how we think and, as a result, into our practice with children in the early years. We know that none of us is purely good or purely bad, but this fact can be overridden by our preconceived beliefs.

A *lack of compassion* can also permeate our practice on a subliminal level, fed by the belief that there will be adverse consequences if black people ever gain equality. This is usually driven by a *perceived threat to identity*. Mainstream society helps to instil these concerns in everyday citizens and then expects them to conform to professional practice that goes against these core beliefs. All of our concerns are valid, and if we do not have responsible ways to express them, then they may filter into our practice in ways that are either not healthy for us or not healthy for a child.

A lack of empathy is a natural occurrence if you don't have any reason to walk in the shoes of another person. It would be so easy to divorce all of this from early years practice because it is so uncomfortable. However, ignoring the existence of racial discord is, in fact, ignoring the establishment of racial hierarchies in society and allowing for these hierarchies to continue to perpetuate and reinforce injustices in society and ultimately in early years practice.

Whilst most white British people may not be able to empathise with the experiences of black people, is anyone ever really, truly colour-blind to race? Racial bias stops us from making an emotional *connection with people who are different to us* as it requires revealing things about "us" that we really don't want "them" to know. *This fear of being vulnerable with "others"* means that there will be very little scope to explore the phenomenon of racism through conversation, understanding, and empathy unless we create safe spaces where we can be vulnerable and express ourselves freely without judgement if we are truly cultivating the idea of change.

I love language and playing with words; creating alliterative phrases is one of my favourite things to do. So here goes! In summing up, what keeps the racism tree alive and well lies in this alliterative equation:

Baseless beliefs + fallacious fear + political power = rampant racism

For this equation to hold true, the opposite must also be true. So, let's test that theory. This could be tricky with my attempts at alliteration, but I am going to give it a whirl:

Objective observation + reasoned response + inclusive influence = sophisticated society

I am so impressed with myself right now! I managed to squeeze some assonance alongside alliteration into my equation! The equation is not perfect but hopefully you get my gist. I have not expressed these experiences for my black and ethnic minority readers to feel sorry for themselves nor to create feelings of pity or shame in my white readers. This is purely to share the black experience through the eyes of a black person. I know for sure that my white, Chinese, and Indian Jamaican friends do not have the same experiences as I do as a black Jamaican. I am also well aware that I can't speak for all black people and there will be some black people who will say that this is not their experience of life in Britain at all, but I would be surprised if they can't relate to anything I have said. It also has to be acknowledged that people process their life experiences in different ways.

- Some people use these experiences to motivate them to succeed in the face of hostility and adversity, no matter how exhausting this might be.
- Some may choose to give up and pursue a life of crime or turn to alcohol or drugs.
- Many just accept their fate and try to navigate life as best as possible.
- And then there are the change makers, those that tirelessly work for a better life for all.

"A whole new world"

Don't even pretend that you don't know the lyrics to *Frozen* inside out! Because of my granddaughter, I have no choice but to have a full-body experience of Elsa, Anna, Olaf, and the rest of the crew! The children in our settings belt out "Let it go" with vigour and affirmation but I have to admit to just having sung along without really paying attention to the lyrics until Myla (my granddaughter) got an Elsa doll that sang the song. I finally paid attention to the lyrics:

My power flurries through the air into the ground
My soul is spiralling in frozen fractals all around
And one thought crystallizes like an icy blast
I'm never going back, the past is in the past

Let it go, let it go
When I'll rise like the break of dawn
Let it go, let it go
That perfect girl is gone
Here I stand in the light of day
Let the storm rage on
The cold never bothered me anyway.

These are powerful lyrics! This is a song about freedom from mental shackles. This resonates with me in regard to being shackled to a concept of "whiteness" to be successful in society. We are told that we need to straighten our hair and dress to make our white colleagues feel comfortable or else succumb to the stereotypes that have been assigned to our "blackness." We look forward to rising anew like the break of dawn by continuing to mentally disempower the historical glass ceilings that seek to confine us, our children, and our young people – glass ceilings that shatter and become frozen fractals that spiral around us when we free ourselves and continue to embrace our blackness and proudly understand and live out loud that our blackness is a gift and not a curse. When my children were younger, *Aladdin* was "the bomb." The DVD was constantly in play, with John and Matt belting out "A whole new world." Again, another set of lyrics I never paid attention to until recently, when watching classic Disney films with Myla. These lyrics took on a whole new meaning for me:

> A whole new world
> A new fantastic point of view
> No one to tell us, "No"
> Or where to go
> Or say we're only dreaming
> A whole new world
> A dazzling place I never knew
> But when I'm way up here
> It's crystal clear
> That now I'm in a whole new world with you.

Can you imagine if all of us who work with young children actively co-created this whole new world with children and parents and each other? Where would we start? I am trying to work through this concept as I am writing, so bear with me. I think I would start with what this whole new world would look and feel like if children were involved in making it and then explore the processes involved in collaborating to design and create this world. I think we would actively create a learning environment where we:

Tune-in to children: by observing more and speaking less.

Ask open-ended questions: and make sure we have strategies in place to hear every child.

Listen: by actively observing for verbal and non-verbal messages and show-
ing attentiveness.
Keep conversations going: with children, parents, staff, and all stakeholders.

Then we would invest time to:

Learn: about the people in our community and their backgrounds and histo-
ries and the things that are important to them.
Expect: the best for every child and actively prepare every child for the international and global workforce of the future.
Appreciate: the cultures of all people even when our cohorts may be predominantly white. This will help to decentralise the concept of whiteness and promote the fact of humanity.
Provide: all children with opportunities that endorse and validate them, not
only culturally but also as unique individuals. No one needs to carry the
burden of racial stereotypes.

(adapted from Anti-Racist Classrooms, Illinois Civics Hub)

As early years professionals it appears we are going to **TALK** and **LEAP**! It
is a good thing that we are used to multi-tasking in our profession, so it's
onwards and upwards with the task of creating this dazzling place we never
knew could exist.

"But what does this look like in practice?"

Have you ever attended training and heard about the most amazing practice and immediately started envisaging the perfect children in perfect settings where practice is seamlessly executed and started wondering whether
there was real advice for real children in a real nursery? Co-creation of
this whole new world will entail the individual child, their physical environment, their social environment, especially parents as co-educators, and, of
course, us as practitioners. For meaningful change to happen, these areas
have to work both independently and inclusively for children. Within our
settings we know that children are thriving from anti-racist practice when,
as practitioners:

- We accomplish paying attention to children of all races as part of our exemplary practice.
- We listen to all children inclusively and truly hear what they say, because although children may come from similar backgrounds, their needs should never be assumed to be generic.
- All the children in our care know that we see them and know them for who they are, and they know that we are "irrationally crazy" about them. I suspect if we open our hearts and minds, we will discover children of all races who are quirky, funny, stoic, quiet and reserved, loud and energetic, rude, rich, poor, middle class, working class, gifted, average, gifted in alternative ways, have skills and abilities that surprise us, have additional needs, medical issues, mental health issues, and so on. None of these attributes belongs to any one race.
- We work with children in a way that values every child "as rich in potential, strong, powerful, competent, and most of all, connected to adults and children" (Malaguzzi, 1997, p. 117). This is the amazing part of working with children and contributing to shaping what the future of the world will be like for all of us. We have the best job in the world: to guide, nurture, teach, and learn about all the children in our care.

An important part of our work in early education as adults is to model sending the message to each and every child that they are valued and they belong. This surely has to be the basis of a good-quality early years curriculum. It is important that educators inform themselves about how *not* to reinforce racial prejudices and how to address these issues with compassion and sensitivity.

THE SPACE FOR INTERACTIVE CHANGE – SEMI-VISIBLE

Questions for reflection:

1. What policies and practices do we have in our settings that demonstrate our remit for treating all children equally?
2. What does equal treatment mean in your setting?

3. If we are displaying unconscious bias, how might this be playing out in our settings?
4. How can you find out if unconscious bias is having a negative effect on children and parents?
5. How can we cultivate professional love as part of our practice with young children?

If we do not challenge ourselves as educators, our learning communities can become infused with negative messages which means some children automatically receive less than their full educational entitlement. Educators could inadvertently create a self-fulfilling prophesy situation, essentially the impact of the negative reinforcement loop we spoke about in the previous chapter. This is a complex interplay between what an early childhood professional expects from a child, and what that child subsequently achieves. There is evidence to suggest that if an early childhood professional expects a child to underachieve, they may provide less encouragement and less challenging tasks, and take less responsibility for that child's learning, hence creating the environment for that prophecy to come true. In many cases, bias held by early childhood professionals towards certain races, cultures, or ability groups is perceived by children and in turn impacts on children's expectations of their own achievement (Kuklinski & Weinstein, 2001).

Learning to be comfortable with being uncomfortable in the process of change

These conversations need to take place if we are ever to shift systemic racism, but *how* these conversations take place matters. They are, by nature, uncomfortable discussions that need to be had with some basic ground rules to ensure that anyone taking part comes away with the conviction to make a change rather than feeling shame and despondency. We already know that shame and empathy do not sit comfortably together in a space for change. Adults are in a strong position to influence children, rightly or wrongly; therefore, if diversity and inclusion are to be addressed in a meaningful way, prejudicial attitudes and behaviours in adults, even when unintentional, need to be addressed constructively. Prejudice, inequality, and oppression have denied too many children and their families access to their equal rights as human beings and to many of life's positive experiences and opportunities. An attitude of checking ourselves and modelling that for children, as well as making a commitment to addressing racism in our learning environments and our curriculum offer, has benefits for the wider community as well. In reviewing our own practice as early years educators, we ensure that we are committed to our remit of advocacy for the children whose lives we touch.

At this point I feel like it is time for the driver to take a break and double-check that the route we are on is still the best one and whether we are still on track and making good progress. I see early years care and education as the beginning of the education phases and, as such, being deeply embedded in the education system. I also believe that addressing systemic racism within early years settings means addressing systemic racism in the entire education system and in society as a whole. Being authentic to my own experiences and the experiences of black people in Britain is my attempt at addressing systemic racism from the "messy" entanglements of human emotions as encouraged by the "Water of Systems Change" framework. This framework also reminds us that successful change is vastly increased by focusing on what is invisible to many, alongside turning the lens on to ourselves. I strongly believe that we cannot divorce human emotion from an issue in which an individual's perception of the "truth" regarding another person is a product of social construction and social conditioning rather than objective observation, especially when systemic racism thrives in a culture of denial which only adds to the confusion from both a personal and professional perspective.

Earlier in the book we spoke about setting goals and being clear on mini-successes in our anti-racist practice journey. If we are on the right track during this journey, the landscape should begin to look like this:

- Professionals in the early years who are trauma-aware and emotionally aware enough to understand whether they are tuned into all children within their care.
- Educators who routinely examine their views, perceptions, and biases and unpick what contributes to how these are formed, as well as fill in gaps in knowledge to counteract the barrage of myths we are all exposed to.

- Educators who are committed to hearing the experiences of black and ethnic minority families who live in a system that is biased against them.
- Communities who are open to hearing the stories of British people who, largely through no fault of their own, may not fully know their history or be really sure that systemic racism even exists.
- Remembering British people who stood out from the crowd and continue to stand out from the crowd, and choosing to speak to them to find out how they are able to be at peace with anti-racism and how they protect their mental space.

I hope that this book motivates educators to uphold a vision of citizenship and an entitlement to equal rights for *all* children, irrespective of circumstance. Increasingly, the freedom to work in this way in education is threatened and becoming even more restricted through governmental policies that promote black people's lived experiences as "victim narratives" whilst continuing to deny the existence of systemic racism. The hidden and generally distorted perspectives of the expectations and the realities of black and ethnic minority people in Britain is historical. Beginning to delve beneath the surface for knowledge and understanding is the "stuff" that brilliant educators and practitioners are made of.

The warning light on the dashboard

"Work on the problem or prepare for the fallout"

When we started this journey, we made sure to pack well for everyone, check how everyone was doing periodically, and carefully factor in the stops to replenish petrol; the one thing we forgot to do was to check the engine. All our best plans for getting to our destination could be foiled by not paying attention to the health of our car engine. If the engine cuts out then it is usually down to fuel, the electric ignition, or the air the engine needs for the internal combustion process. These issues can generally be fixed easily. If, however, warning lights start flashing on your dashboard then this may be as a result of issues with lubrication, the cooling system, or synchronisation in the vehicle control system. These issues could result in damage to the car's engine.

I used to joke that I drove a self-fixing car when I was younger because I would ignore the amber warning light, which then developed into strange noises and excessive smoke, indicating that something was seriously wrong with my car's engine. I was petrified of what it would cost to fix the problem so as long as the light was amber, I drove the car without getting it fixed. Luckily, with my husband's help (he was horrified about the state of my car), I was able to upgrade my vehicle so I never had to experience the red warning light. The thing is, I was always stressed that something disastrous would happen and I can definitely say that not knowing was not worth the stress nor the ongoing damage to the car. Well, the amber warning light came on a while back and now there are some strange noises and excessive smoke as well; we really should stop and get the car seen to because continuing like this will certainly have serious implications for us all reaching our destination safely. We have to weigh up if everyone arriving safely at their

DOI: 10.4324/9781003247807-6

destination is worth the cost and the investment involved in ensuring that the car is in a good driving condition.

Each of us has a decision to make about the children in our care: is it ok in the grand scheme of things to sacrifice the future of some children who are black because after all, black ethnic groups only make up 3.3 per cent of the total population in England? And only 9.5 per cent of the black population in Britain are children aged 0 to 4 years old. If the government in power operates and justifies making decisions that mainly benefit the majority, is it then reasonable that this small minority of children can be sacrificed for "the greater good"? Allow me to break this down in real terms: that 9.5 per cent of black people who are aged 0 to 4 years old is equivalent to 176,849 real children that live in Britain! Is it still ok to view them as dispensable as long as the system works for the majority of white British children? We know that ignoring the health, wellbeing, and education of 176,849 children under five years old puts a strain on social systems which affects all of us in society despite our race. Should we continue ignoring the amber light that has now turned red or should we act before it is too late?

Adverse childhood experiences

I know that, as early years professionals, we understand child development and how adverse childhood experiences (ACEs) can derail healthy growth and development in children. However, it is very easy to externalise these adverse experiences as something that happens to children outside of their early years settings. What if I told you that early years professionals can also be responsible, unknowingly, and sometimes knowingly? Childhood adversity is heavily focused on the effects of negative family experiences on a child's personal development but seemingly disregards the impact of professional personality factors. Negative societal attitudes and biases saturate all facets of a child's ecology, and they persist over time; so, as early years professionals, we cannot ignore the importance of these factors on long-term outcomes for ethnic minority children. Persistent exposure to racial discrimination and structural racism leads to psychological distress which, as we know, without social buffering and supportive adults in a child's life, will clearly affect the developing brain.

Back in Chapter 3 we spoke about typical patterns of child development, and we know that one of the periods when the brain is susceptible to change is between 0 and 5 years old. Adverse childhood experiences can result in both short- and long-term negative life-changing circumstances in care, health, education, criminal justice, job prospects, and life expectancy outcomes. Is there any justification that will ever make it acceptable to produce childhood trauma in the systems that are supposed to protect all young children? As professionals who adhere to professional standards in our field of expertise, can we continue to ignore the persistent negative social ecology that exists for some children? Let us look more closely at the metaphors we use in early childhood practice to explain child development and the negative implications for later learning if children are consistently deprived of these responses by the adults who should be nurturing and supporting them.

Serve and return

"Serve and return" is a tennis metaphor that describes the "rally" interactions between young children and the adults in their lives. The child "serves" by reaching out for interaction through babbling, facial expressions, and gestures and adults "return" by speaking, playing peek-a-boo, and sharing a toy, for example. These interactions are crucial for cognitive and linguistic development and are essentially the building blocks of early brain development. Research tells us that positive nurturing relationships help children to learn how to control their emotions, take turns, and manage stress. Children who are consistently ignored are, in no uncertain terms, suffering from neglect, and over time this failure to "return their serve" weakens their brain architecture and impairs their development of skills and abilities for later learning as well as contributing to a negative impact on health and behaviour.

I know what reaching out and being ignored feels like from my most recent stay in hospital when I had Covid pneumonia. It literally hurts! That feeling of having no control over the situation you are in and that you are not worthy of attention is soul-destroying. As an adult I experienced emotional trauma as a result of nine days of being in an environment which was generally lacking in care and understanding, apart from the odd "saviours" who would turn up and leave again. (I am entirely grateful for the few "saviours" who helped me to survive this experience but the disparity in practice, which was definitely race-based, only served to highlight how disturbingly dysfunctional the NHS is. Bad practice seemed permissable as long as it was happening to a black person. My experience only became worse when a complaint was raised by another patient about the treatment I received. Even as an educated black woman, I am now petrified about becoming ill and vulnerable in a system where I felt as if I was expendable.) This was an environment that denied me emotional responsiveness when I needed it most. The experience affected me so intensely that the idea of young children having to experience similar feelings for up to five days a week, nine to twelve hours a day is just overwhelming.

Let us take this away from race for a moment, to something that is far more relatable for anyone who has ever experienced or even heard about relationships where one partner frequently resorts to "the silent treatment." Think about what this does to the person who is consistently on the receiving end of this treatment:

- Makes them feel angry, sad, unworthy, unloved, resentful, ashamed, guilty – rollercoaster of emotions – emotional trauma.
- Causes stress and anxiety.
- Lowers self-worth and self-esteem.
- Creates self-doubt and changes in their behaviour.
- Leads to mental health issues and medical issues.
- Leads them to become anxiously attached – needy.
- Makes them feel out of control in the situation.
- Leaves them feeling confused, uncertain, hopeless.

Most young black children carry around these feelings to some degree. They have these same feelings but without the words to express how they feel; so, they could either cry out for attention or they could also become eerily quiet, which is something that is easily overlooked in a busy early years environment. The quiet child who does not present as a problem to the practitioner can become embroiled in a cycle of being ignored which will result in long-term psychological damage.

I remember my granddaughter at three years old telling me that she felt hurt because I was too busy to play with her. I was grateful she had the words to express herself and I promised her there and then that "girls' time" would be free of the distractions of my phone or my computer or all the other "adult" things I had to do; it would just be time for both of us. I have kept that promise: we have spa dates, cake-baking dates, Lego-building and imaginative-play dates, Minecraft creative-mode dates, dance-party dates, drive-around dates where she gets to pick the direction we drive in, and more. The point being: she is confident, self-assured, adventurous, intelligent, creative, curious, and eager to learn. I dread the thought that someone could knowingly or unknowingly do her emotional harm in her educational journey by subjecting her to a systematic pattern of negative interactions purely because of the colour of her skin.

As early years professionals, it is essential for us to label the harm and to unpack emotional maltreatment of children, especially as it is often not transparent. A high standard of ethical consideration is needed within our early years learning environments to ensure that no child is exposed to this level of harm by adults who should be nurturing and supporting them in their learning and development. An ethical obligation to intervene when children are experiencing emotional maltreatment should be second nature in all early years environments.

The stress metaphor

Stress is the body's reaction to feeling under pressure; however, not all stress is bad. Positive stress can be a motivator for problem-solving. During natural disasters, for example, if a child gets injured or a loved one dies, stress can be made tolerable by the positive, supportive relationships provided by caregivers, who are able to help turn down the stress response. Toxic or harmful stress, on the other hand, occurs when a child experiences prolonged exposure to abuse or neglect and does not have enough support to turn off the stress response. In the early years we are very good at identifying abuse and neglect when it comes from the home environment but not so much when it occurs in the learning environment, unless it is overt and extreme, or it hits the media. Toxic stress is just as devastating when it is experienced as emotional maltreatment in a learning environment where a child does not feel safe or supported; this is the case for a lot of young black children.

Allow me to stick with the pattern of relating to adult situations out of the context of race. Imagine you work as a PA in an advertising firm and five minutes before the team meeting every morning your boss sends you out for coffee, which makes you late for every meeting. If you use your initiative to bring coffee in with you, he complains that he really fancied a caramel macchiato that morning instead of his usual Americano. On top of everything, he repeatedly calls you a "slowpoke" and openly berates you for your tardiness; now everyone thinks it's funny to make jokes about you being "late for your own funeral." Throughout the day your boss constantly reprimands and ridicules you and takes credit for your work. You are at breaking point, but you need this job. Think about the effects on this PA who has this to look forward to every day:

- Feeling singled out, spurned, belittled, shamed, and humiliated.
- Feeling isolated.
- Feeling over-pressured and exploited.
- Being set up to fail.
- Living in fear of what each day will present.
- Feeling a lack of support from colleagues who are just relieved that they are not the target of the boss' treatment.

If a child is in a learning environment where there is no physical abuse but emotional maltreatment is prolific, then this list of effects is what creates the damage to mental health that these children will need to overcome to fulfil their learning and life potential. We can never underestimate the power of the education system in indoctrinating some children into a sense of inferiority, making them doubt their abilities and causing a steady erosion of their self-worth. I believe that because this process is slow and instinctive it allows for a nulling of any real acknowledgement or responsibility for the damage it causes. Think of the apologue that describes a frog being boiled alive slowly; when the water is tepid, no danger is perceived, and the slow, systematic, and incremental turning up of the heat is a metaphor for the unwillingness or inability of early years professionals to see the part they play in systematically eroding the life chances of some children.

Air traffic control

Children learn to organise their "executive functions" very similarly to how an air traffic controller organises and manages planes taking off and landing in a busy airport. Those of us who are blessed to have supportive adults in our lives generally learn the mental skills that help us to pay attention, control our impulses, process information, prioritise tasks, and plan, organise, and manage our time. Issues with executive function can affect everything from interacting with other people to the ability to learn and work productively. Trauma and life events can weaken the metabolic processes of the brain. A child who is emotionally overwhelmed and overly stressed is in fight, flight, or freeze mode. Children are hardwired to observe patterns in their world, and as they develop, they begin to ascribe meaning to these patterns. Being consistently treated in harmful or negative ways produces a trauma response in young children that, without the right kind of support, can impact on their ability to learn and function at certain levels even as adults.

Again, let's remove the dynamic of race and project the scenario into adulthood. Imagine landing a job as a social scientist, a job that will make a real difference for many people. However, you basically got the job because the company director is a family friend. Despite your intellectual capability, you have poor impulse control, you find it difficult to stay on task, you have weakened working memory and attention skills, you can't process a lot of information coming from multiple people, and your organisational skills and time management is poor. You don't really like being around people and you work best when you are left alone to work at your own pace and within your own time, but this is a job that demands collaboration and results to generate funding. Think about the impact on this person:

- Feeling overwhelmed.
- Feeling anxious.
- Feeling frustrated.
- Being forgetful.
- Lashing out or withdrawing.
- Being unable to manage and filter distractions.
- Being unable to follow rules and instructions.
- Being unable to manage competing demands.

Imagine being a child who feels and functions in this way, a child whose poor executive function is blamed on race and circumstances with no acknowledgement of how systemic inequalities add to childhood trauma. If a child's learning environment consistently lacks a stable routine; calm, supportive practitioners; time to practice, play, problem-solve; opportunities to develop their identity and cultivate self-awareness and confidence; then the education system is responsible for negatively impacting on the acquisition of fundamentally important executive function skills that are an active part of early childhood development. The education system then also has to bear responsibility for churning out citizens who, later on in life, will work with constantly elevated stress levels and who may be unable to work productively in roles that they are more than intellectually capable of fulfilling.

Overloaded

A lorry that is overloaded to the point of breaking down is the metaphor that is usually used to describe how issues such as neglect can factor into the lives of ethnic minority children. However, the concept of being "overloaded" is a double-edged sword: it also speaks to societal issues that can overload parents' mental and emotional capacity and erode their ability to take care of their children. Because the clinical aspects of the impact of dysregulated emotions in children appear to be little explored outside the medical field, it is perhaps hard to understand how the education system contributes to this particular adverse childhood experience. As early years professionals, it is important to realise that parents being overloaded by societal circumstances does not mean that they are not doing their absolute best to be good parents. Technically, most parents just need some support to lighten or manage the load to get the lorry back on the road in good working order. It has to be acknowledged that there are extreme cases, which tend to be part of the cycle of discrimination grounded in multi-systemic failures, which can lead to chronic anti-social behaviours and negative outcomes for young children, and so on in a vicious circle. Dysregulated emotions in children need far more professional scrutiny and intervention; and for a black child and a black family there should be the same investment, in terms of lightening or managing the load, that a white child and a white family are likely to routinely receive. Remember, these children become adults, who have children, and so the cycle continues.

Emotions are underpinned by psychological and physiological mechanisms that allow children to regulate themselves when external and internal challenges are experienced. Unfortunately, these mechanisms can become dysregulated for various reasons, including due to environmental factors. Societal issues such as systemic racism contribute to emotional overload that leads to long-term wear and tear of the brain and the body. We know that the element of "self" is central to good mental health and psychological wellbeing and we know that positive and negative childhood experiences influence children's abilities to perform well in the early years and in further education.

Early years professionals can never underestimate their influence on a child's development of a sense of self. The case studies in Chapter 5 highlight the constant stressful, anxiety-provoking situations that black children and adults experience on a daily basis, inside and outside of the education system. People who experience this level of repeated trauma can become limited in their ability to perceive the situations they are in as manageable challenges rather than imminent threats. Emotional regulation involves the use of cognitive skills to challenge interpretations and reframe meaning to enable up- or down-regulation in emotional responses to situations. When the situation is constant and systemic in nature this results in dysregulated emotions. From previous chapters, we can already understand this in terms of brain function and a pattern of circumstances that impedes the pre-frontal cortex from doing its job to calm the amygdala down.

In keeping with our previous examples: Joe finds it difficult to hold down employment; he has high levels of shame and anger and suffers from undiagnosed anxiety and depression, but feels it is not "manly" to be treated for these issues. Instead, he resorts to excessive use of alcohol and recreational drugs, which impacts on his home relationships as well as his state of mind when he is at work. Joe has frequent angry outbursts at work, which have resulted in his colleagues steering clear of him, and he often complains of feeling rejected, ignored, and judged. He feels stressed and "caged in" at work, lacks motivation, and regularly makes poor decisions. Joe constantly repeats the pattern of walking out on a job or being fired from it. He has normalised his early childhood trauma which manifested as:

- Deprivation of his basic childhood care needs both at home and in education.
- Failure of adequate supervision at home and in his learning environment.
- Disregard for his emotional, social, and educational needs.
- Persistent levels of covert and overt invalidation.

Every time I have ever met a "Joe" outside of brain-injury situations, I see the child who has become broken by their childhood trauma. It would be very easy to assume that black children and adults who operate with a heightened stress and threat level do so purely because of dysregulated emotions and an inherent lack of ability to manage challenge. However, childhood ecology has a major part to play. Early years education is the beginning of the journey of finding your sense of identity, and this is largely determined by a sense of belonging. It is important that young children's conceptions of their identities allow them to believe that education holds value for them. If they learn to believe that people who speak their language and look like them are not intelligent or capable, then they will act according to that belief. When children are stereotyped, academic performance deteriorates. They experience anxiety, physiological stress, reduced capacity of working memory, and a drain on their cognitive resources. As educators, we need to make it a priority to create an environment where children thrive and there are no limits to them achieving their full potential. Research has shown that further academic outcomes, such as motivation, dropout rates, and academic performance, are correlated with feelings of belonging.

THE SPACE FOR STRUCTURAL CHANGE – VISIBLE

Questions for reflection:

1. How comfortable do our black and ethnic minority colleagues feel about aspiring for career progression in the workplace?
2. If black leadership is non-existent in your work environments, and the only black staff in your work environments are the cleaners, what are the unspoken messages to children and families in your learning community?

If at this point you are feeling a bit overwhelmed about the intricacy of systemic racism and where to start the journey towards anti-racist practice, then I have another Jamaican saying for you: "yu haffi slice de bread fi eat it." To be fair, you could break off bits of the bread instead of slicing it, but you get what I am saying; we have to start by making a start and by dealing with the process through smaller manageable actions. I love these other bread quotes as well: "Everyone is kneaded out of the same dough but not baked in the same oven" (Yiddish proverb) and "We have learned to see in bread an instrument of community between men – the flavour of bread shared has no equal" (Antoine de Saint-Exupery). All these references to bread serve to remind us of the power of sharing a meal in getting to really know others. We do this in our dating lives, and we know the value of eating with children as keyworkers, and if we extend this to planned events with parents and invest in the **TALK/LEAP** strategy during these times, we would actually be in the process of shifting our perception from fear to love. Love unleashes our power to co-create because it harnesses our collective vision and expands it into a place of abundance and wellbeing for all.

The power of professional love
Working above and beyond our biases

Practitioners in the early years know, without a shadow of a doubt, that care and education are inextricably linked. In my opinion this dynamic never really changes, even when children become more self-sufficient; the level of care just becomes less physically hands-on as children become more independent. As we have said many times before, children thrive when they feel that they belong, especially when that belonging comes from a place of emotional warmth from the adults in their lives. The use of the word *love* in a professional capacity can be quite uncomfortable, especially in the early years when we can be preoccupied with safeguarding practices and possible allegations of inappropriateness. So we spend hours trying to find safer words that say *love* without actually saying *love*. The concept of professional love was created by Dr Jools Page, who coined the phrase to explain the difference between parental love and professional love. A child's emotional needs do not stop when they come into our settings and professional love does not ever replace parental love; it simply extends the loving support of comfort and reassurance that children need to flourish. Professional love is an interesting concept because it comes with the discernment to vary how this love is manifested in order to meet the needs of individual children who are all unique individuals. Professional love has those boundaries that come with our roles in working in the early years, but when you think and act from a place of love as an essential aspect of the practices and processes in our settings, the best outcomes are possible for *all* children.

Do you remember the feeling of being overwhelmed that we spoke about at the end of Chapter 6? Well, once we start seeing the world through the lens of professional love, our eyes, minds, and hearts become open to the signs we used to miss and suddenly the path for going forward lights

DOI: 10.4324/9781003247807-7

up before us. This does not mean that we will never stumble or fall but the amazing part of walking this journey with others is that you are not alone. There will always be someone to help us up. When we co-create this new world in the way that we spoke about earlier, we come together as a group of different people with different perspectives and work together to creatively develop strategies for our defined challenge of anti-racist practice within our settings. We become focused on a way of working that is:

- Human-centred.
- Mindful of the experiences of children, staff, and parents.
- Constantly valuing the collaboration of children, parents, staff, and stakeholders.

I genuinely believe co-creation to be fundamental to our world becoming more empathetic, more interconnected, and more humane and I know from experience that the combination of professional love and co-creation is powerful in anti-racist practice because it incrementally and consistently shifts the dynamic. For the rest of this final chapter, I am going to focus on linking strategies to theory and sharing some examples from my own practice that have made a real difference in implementing anti-racist practice in our setting.

STORY TIME: SOME OF MY EXPERIENCES AS A BLACK EARLY YEARS LEADER

In human culture, storytelling is a long-established tradition. People tell stories for all kinds of reasons – to entertain, to share knowledge, to pass on information and traditions, to maintain cultural heritage, or simply to warn others of danger. It is clear that a fundamental aspect of storytelling is based in human emotion. The basic beliefs and values of people and groups are projected into stories. Stories teach us how to live, how to behave, and stories are dynamic. Stories are told about individuals, groups, communities, cultures, societies, and nations and they are a powerful leadership tool and also a powerful learning tool in our profession as early years practitioners. As human beings we are programmed for stories. They're a part of who we are. It's how we evolved to understand our place in the world before we had written language. I love the brain and how it works; essentially our brains run on electrical pulses that light up when we connect to stories. When our neurons are triggered in this way it helps us to remember more of the information we are receiving. So, with that in mind, it's story time.

Power and the "feel-good factor"

We need to have realistic expectations of leading a racially inclusive early years environment; with the best will in the world, not everyone can "gel" with it. In my first year of working with this ethos, I lost four members of staff despite the safe, non-judgemental spaces for dialogue, the supervision, the peer support, and working more with parents in a more inclusive manner. One member of staff told me that she had always enjoyed her job before I came, that she used to "feel good" and that the parents were always grateful to her. The issue for me, in observing her practice, was that how she interacted with parents and children was very power-based. The parents knew their place and were made to feel grateful for her attention, so changing the tone of relationships with parents to where they were valued as co-educators was very challenging for her, especially when parents started communicating with her from a position of equal value. The work environment lost "the feel-good factor" for her when relationships with children and parents, who were predominantly non-white, became more equal.

"Who are *you* to make *me* feel bad?"

An older member of staff felt that she held all her good practice in her head and knew instinctively what to do with children. My observations of her showed that she did not even know the names of the children and the reports she wrote about children's progress seemed to be more about quickly dispensing with the responsibility of having to write a report than actually producing something that bore any resemblance to the children she had been teaching for a whole year. She actually said that the teachers in the primary school do not read the progress reports anyway so it was a waste of her time and also, if she had wanted to spend her time doing planning, observation, and assessment, she would have gone to work in a predominantly middle class area of Birmingham such as Sutton Coldfield! I was gobsmacked! That was such a loaded statement, but her bias was so deeply embedded that she had no idea of the implications behind what she had said. When I asked her if only children in areas like Sutton Coldfield are entitled to a high level of professional practice, she dissolved into tears and accused me of trying to make her feel bad. She retired at the end of that summer term, and she did not hold back in letting everyone know that she was not yet ready to retire but she felt she needed to go because "people like her [meaning me!] come along and try to change up everything and make people like me [meaning her] feel bad."

"The rough kind"

Regular supervisions with staff are a part of my leadership practice. After years of working with a particular member of staff, one day during his supervision he suddenly told me that when I was first recruited, he had somehow got to know about it before everyone else so he had gone around telling everyone that "one of the rough kind" was coming to work in the school. At this point he was apologising for thinking of me in that way without knowing me, and he was also thanking me for the support I had given to him as a young practitioner. While I was a little surprised at being stereotyped as being "one of the rough kind," I wasn't shocked by it. I chose instead to focus on his growth, and I appreciated the fact that he felt comfortable enough to confess this to me even though he did not have to. The truth is, I had already heard about this years before, but never in a million years did I ever expect him to tell me of his own accord. My respect for him really grew.

Motivation to do and courage to withstand

One of the ways that I build and sustain a shared vision with staff is by carrying out anonymous surveys. They are anonymous because, in my opinion, what staff have to say is far more important than who says it. The first time I did this was actually quite hard as I had to deal with some very hurtful things that were said, including staff who were very open about not wanting a black person as a leader in their setting and some very personal comments that, quite frankly, blew me away. It took me about a week to not internalise this, and then I worked on producing a document which each member of staff received, reporting the raw findings of the survey with their comments and analysing the comments against our situation.

On the positive side, I was able to adapt some of our practice with some really helpful suggestions from staff and it was actually a really powerful experience for all. Staff mentioned they knew the survey was real when they were able to read their own comments; there was an expression of deep shock in regard to some of the racist comments and one member of staff spoke up and said that though it was alarming to see the comments on paper, it really made her think about how these feelings are generally kept hidden. This was the start of us devising ways of working together to learn more about each other as people, which was hugely rewarding for our practice with children and parents as well.

"Bad to the bone – well it's genetic, isn't it?"

I remember constantly hearing a child's name just being bellowed by staff day after day. He was the one little black boy in the class at the time and to be fair, he was high-spirited. This resulted in him being called out for anything and everything that was negative in the class. At the point where I intervened, I observed that children had picked up on this and would make up stories about him just for him to be shouted at. Parents were frequently complaining about not wanting their child to be in the same room as this little boy. I spoke to his mum, who said to me that she dreaded picking him up after nursery because, every day, she was greeted with how "bad" he was, which translated to her as how bad a parent she was. It had gotten to the point where she was so frustrated that she actually beat him with a belt, but that hadn't helped either as she ended up crying because of how awful she felt. She told me that she was afraid to tell anyone how bad it was because she was afraid "they would take her child away from her."

I will never forget how tired, stressed, and afraid this mum was, and she confided in me that if I hadn't approached her, she never would have felt comfortable coming forward. I explored the things that triggered his behaviour with his mum, and I discovered that it had a lot to with his diet and his beleaguered mother who was struggling to manage with three children all under the age of five. Between the school and his mum we started managing the things that contributed to him acting up, including his diet, providing more challenging activities so he was not bored, giving him more responsibility, which helped him to manage his own behaviour, and focusing on and calling out his good behaviour. Slowly he began to change, and we could all see him for the delightful, funny, clever child that he was.

I had two visitors just before lockdown in early 2020: a tall, well-mannered 16-year-old and his mother. He had asked his mother to stop by to look for me; he told me that he has never forgotten us and that he wanted to come to show me that he was doing well. I can never tell this story without crying; he was three years old when we were working with him, but he still remembered us at 16 years old. This was a stark reminder for me that if our interactions with children are not positive, they will still remember us for the rest of their lives but for the wrong reasons.

"What about the children we don't take to?"

This may be an explosive thing to admit, but during my many years of working as a teacher I have met children for whom only the deepest reserves of professional love helped to build a bridge to enable a relationship that worked in the best interest of the child. So how do we train ourselves professionally to think the best of every child, even the ones we do not naturally take to? I would suggest that we should:

- Purposefully note and manage our behaviour towards the children we find irritating or disruptive.

- Be positively vigilant and recognise when the children who challenge us the most are doing the right thing.
- Recognise and acknowledge if our treatment of a child is driven by things they can't change about themselves – their skin colour, hair, disability, illness, status, background, etc.
- Stand back and look at our room and our practice. What does our practice say about us? Does it say that we are we welcoming of *all* children? Does our learning environment subliminally value some children over others? Do parents feel included? Do we have high expectations of some children but not others? Does our practice expose an unconscious perception of other people's cultures as inferior to our own, and how is this manifested?

I want to be that practitioner who will see beyond everything that society says is reasonable and logical to expect for any child; the practitioner who will challenge myself to always make the effort to be cognisant of my impact on every child I come across; the practitioner who will push the boundaries to be a positive force in the lives of all children in my care, even the ones for whom I do not have a natural affinity.

THE SPACE FOR STRUCTURAL CHANGE – VISIBLE

Questions for reflection:

1. How can we centre identity and culture in our practice?
2. Are there any voices or perspectives missing in the development of our early years curriculum? How can we address this?
3. How do we embed the continuous process of self-assessment into our practice?
4. Discuss the difference between "tolerance of others" as opposed to "acceptance of all" and how we can demonstrate this in our practice.
5. How do we create conditions for even our very young children to challenge inequality?

Some strategies and frameworks to support change

4S bubble framework

I created a framework that translates "The Water of Systems Change" into a leadership tool to address the segments that work towards implementing anti-racist practice; see Diagram 7.1 below.

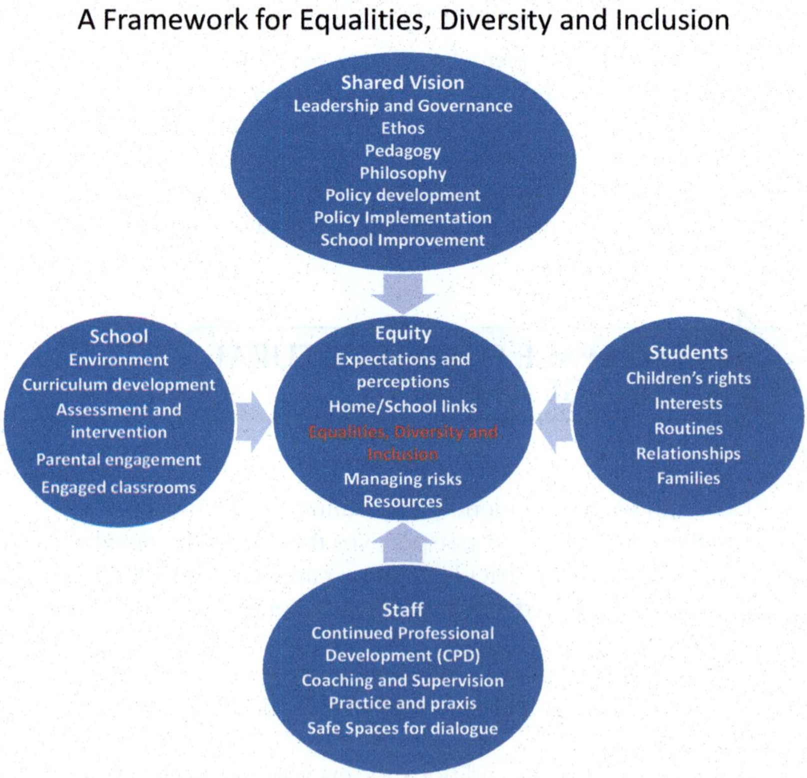

A Framework for Equalities, Diversity and Inclusion

Shared Vision
Leadership and Governance
Ethos
Pedagogy
Philosophy
Policy development
Policy Implementation
School Improvement

School
Environment
Curriculum development
Assessment and intervention
Parental engagement
Engaged classrooms

Equity
Expectations and perceptions
Home/School links
Equalities, Diversity and Inclusion
Managing risks
Resources

Students
Children's rights
Interests
Routines
Relationships
Families

Staff
Continued Professional Development (CPD)
Coaching and Supervision
Practice and praxis
Safe Spaces for dialogue

Diagram 7.1 4S bubble framework.

This framework was made for the wider educational system, hence the reference to school. For early years practice we can substitute "setting" for "school." The diagram has four bubbles that each have an "S" heading (Shared vision, School/Setting, Students, Staff) which are aspects of the early years environment. These 4 "S"s coalesce at the mid-point "Equity" bubble which has equality, diversity, and inclusion at the centre point. This could sit alongside "The Water of Systems Change" as a leadership strategy for working through the process of change towards anti-racist practice in our settings.

The EYFS

As practitioners we do not have to look too far to be reminded of our remit for working with children. The Early Years Foundation Stage (EYFS) Curriculum reminds us that our focus is the unique child, positive relationships, and enabling environments that inform the learning and development of children. The EYFS has been revised, but these guiding principles hold firm for shaping our practice in the early years (Diagram 7.2).

Diagram 7.2 is taken from the previous Development Matters (2012) practice guide, and some of the wording has been changed, but the ethos remains the same. I particularly like this version because it is explicit in valuing all people, being warm and loving, fostering a sense of belonging, valuing and respecting all children and families equally, and stimulating resources relevant to all children's cultures and communities. All children need to see themselves and their families reflected positively in their learning environments. However, it is important that we create an awareness of what might feel like tokenism, stereotyping, or negative connotations associated with perceiving something different as either "exotic" or "inferior" rather than an alternative way of being with respect to us all being unique. I am a little bit sad that these principles did not remain as explicit in the revised 2021 version in regard to anti-racist practice in the early years.

The UN Convention on the Rights of the Child

In our school we actively embed a rights-based educational approach as an underpinning principle in our curriculum development alongside the EYFS;

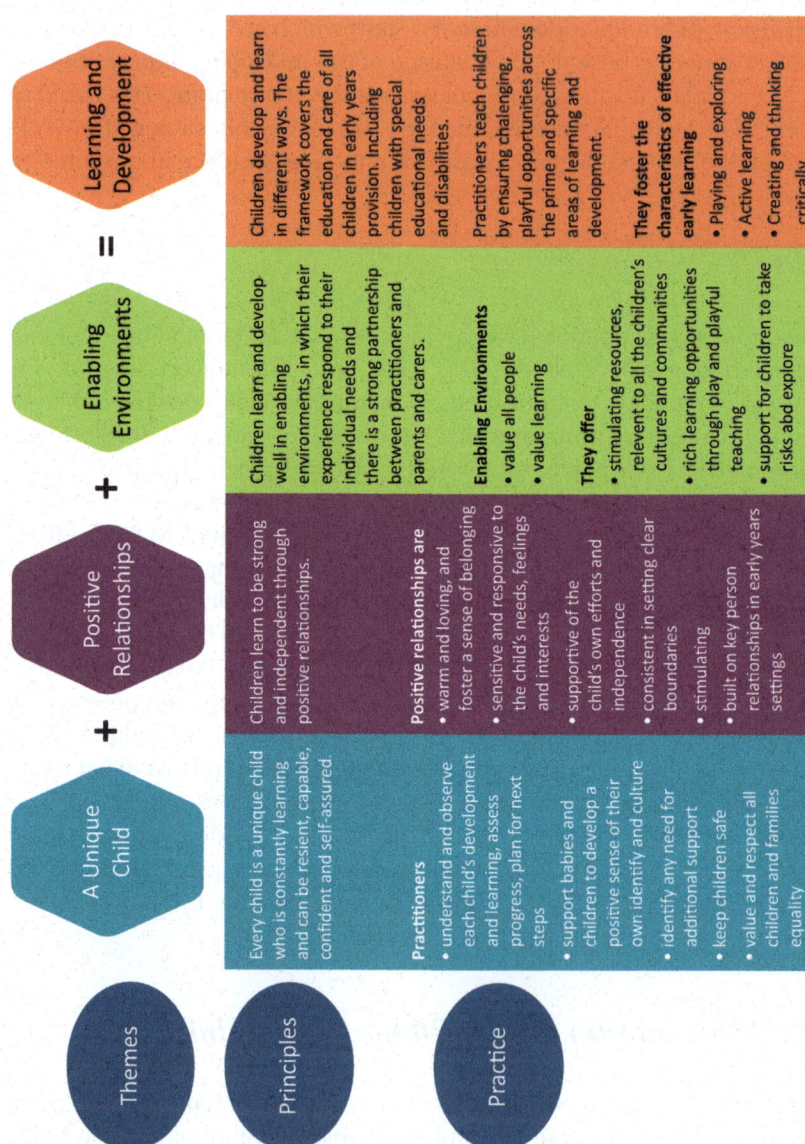

Themes

A Unique Child + Positive Relationships + Enabling Environments = Learning and Development

Principles

A Unique Child

Every child is a unique child who is constantly learning and can be resient, capable, confident and self-assured.

Positive Relationships

Children learn to be strong and independent through positive relationships.

Enabling Environments

Children learn and develop well in enabling environments, in which their experience respond to their individual needs and there is a strong partnership between practitioners and parents and carers.

Learning and Development

Children develop and learn in different ways. The framework covers the education and care of all children in early years provision. Including children with special educational needs and disabilities.

Practice

Practitioners

• understand and observe each child's development and learning, assess progress, plan for next steps
• support babies and children to develop a positive sense of their own identify and culture
• identify any need for additional support
• keep children safe
• value and respect all children and families equality

Positive relationships are

• warm and loving, and foster a sense of belonging
• sensitive and responsive to the child's needs, feelings and interests
• supportive of the child's own efforts and independence
• consistent in setting clear boundaries
• stimulating
• built on key person relationships in early years settings

Enabling Environments

• value all people
• value learning

They offer

• stimulating resources, relevent to all the children's cultures and communities
• rich learning opportunities through play and playful teaching
• support for children to take risks abd explore

Practitioners teach children by ensuring challenging, playful opportunities across the prime and specific areas of learning and development.

They foster the characteristics of effective early learning

• Playing and exploring
• Active learning
• Creating and thinking critically

Diagram 7.2 Overarching principles of the EYFS.

122

essentially, we underpin our practice with the UN Convention on the Rights of the Child, which has 54 articles in total. There are four articles known as the "General Principles" which help to interpret all the other articles and have a key role in how we manage children's rights. These are:

- Best interests of the child (Article 3).
- Right to life, survival, and development (Article 6).
- Right to be heard (Article 12).
- Non-discrimination (Article 2).

As a setting, we work towards the bronze, silver, and gold UNICEF awards; this is really less about the award and more about keeping us focused on embedding a children's rights–based approach in our practice.

The International Baccalaureate – Primary Years Programme

We also use the International Baccalaureate (IB) alongside the EYFS to structure and clarify how we develop learning opportunities that keep us connected to the world. The International Baccalaureate Primary Years Programme (PYP) was introduced in 1997. The PYP model covers age range 3 to 12 years. The IB models are interdisciplinary (relating to more than one branch of knowledge) and multidisciplinary (combining or involving several academic disciplines in an approach to a topic or problem), but most importantly the PYP is transdisciplinary. It takes into consideration how young children learn, and it employs a fluidity in learning across, between, and beyond disciplines. A transdisciplinary approach to curriculum development dissolves the boundaries between education and life and organises teaching and learning around the construction of meaning in the context of real-world problems or themes. Transdisciplinary learning environments do not compartmentalise learning, but rather explore content within the context of inquiry. For example, when we are working with the theme "Where we are in place and time" children might compare and contrast characteristics of houses around the world or they could explore what children around the world see on their journeys to nursery. There are six themes within the PYP:

- Who we are.
- Where we are in place and time.
- How we express ourselves.
- How the world works.
- How we organise ourselves.
- Sharing the planet.

We know that young children experience the world through relationships, and these relationships affect all aspects of their development: physical, social, emotional, intellectual, behavioural, and moral. The quality and the stability of the human relationships a child encounters in their early years is the basis of either a healthy or a high-risk ecology. These relationships actively influence healthy or unhealthy human development. They help children to define who they are and their aspirations, and also help them to understand how and why they are valued by other human beings. Black and ethnic minority children are routinely deprived of healthy relationships due to racial discrimination, which, over the last 70 years in the UK, has impacted the way black children, especially, engage in the human community and, in turn, occupy their place in society. The IB provides us with numerous opportunities for all children to engage in the human community in a positive way. In our school we have discovered that these themes work seamlessly with the EYFS and also keep us grounded in how we relate to each other no matter where we are from. The interconnectedness of the IB programme is depicted in Diagram 7.3.

Navigating the space for structural change

Quality in early years care and education is usually defined in terms of ratios, group size, resources, the curriculum, and, of course, the expertise of the practitioners. The expertise of practitioners is usually measured more by whether a child shows some progress in cognitive development in the "here and now" and far less on the powerful influence the practitioner relationship can have on the life of a child beyond the setting and way into their future. In the early years we are burdened with the mantra of "school readiness," as in whether we have made children "ready" for school (in all honesty I am usually more concerned about whether schools are ready for children, but I digress). We know that school readiness is far more than just literacy and numeracy skills;

Diagram 7.3 Primary Years Programme model.

it is about a child's capacity to form and sustain relationships with teachers, children, and other adults and whether they are moving into school life having been fortified by a healthy ecology that allows them to develop the social and emotional skills that underpin their readiness to learn. Without anti-racist practice, a lot of black children will not receive the social and emotional skills that foster their dispositions for learning in a positive way.

The concept of a safe space in anti-racist practice

Throughout this book I have mentioned the concept of safe spaces. A "safe space" is not a physical location. It is an agreement to commit to consistently providing a supportive, respectful learning and working environment for all involved. Safe spaces help to combat moral relativism, which can manifest as variance in standards as it applies to different communities of people and their cultures. We generally work in environments where people do not feel safe to speak up about their feelings or about anything they perceive as unfair, but we know that in productive and successful learning and working environments employees need to feel included and that their beliefs and values are heard and understood. Leaders in the early years are very aware that

> early educator work environments are children's learning environments: children depend on educators who are not only skilled, but have their well-being and needs supported, too. Just as children's environments can support or impede their learning, teachers' work environments can promote or hinder teachers' practice and ongoing skill development.
>
> (Schlieber and McLean, 2020)

Dynamic anti-racist practice comes about when we see and acknowledge diversity and we create safe spaces to accommodate and challenge each other and grow in understanding together; without this deeper commitment to connect with each other, knowledge is gained in the absence of understanding.

A safe space environment does not insulate us from personality clashes and conflicts; it just gives us an agreed strategy for dealing with these issues and helps us to become more self-aware. In addition, it allows us to understand how we impact on others and, ultimately, how to manage ourselves to make that impact a positive one. As a setting, we devise protocols together for our different safe space activities and if there are any residual, nagging feelings after the activities then we agree that the issue needs to be raised during supervision. In supervision, we either reach a compromise and a clear course of action for our next steps or we agree to disagree but commit to checking on the issue in future supervisions if need be. Some of our safe space activities have been very powerful in shifting our anti-racist practice. For best effect we carry out these activities at various times throughout the year, but I have to admit that with budget constraints and cutting back on everything, we have had to resort to fewer activities and focus more on the ones that give the greatest return.

Safe space activities

The intensive listening exercise

The aim of this exercise is to develop deep listening so as to clearly understand what is being said by the other person. Before you respond, you are asked to think about how to reframe what they have said; starting with the phrase "What I am hearing is …" and ending with "Am I right?," you then tell them what you understand they have said. The other person then has a chance to confirm your understanding or, if you have misunderstood them, clarify what they have said. This exercise is not as easy as it sounds, especially as people always seem to want to respond or defend themselves without checking that they have really understood what they are hearing. However, this has been a powerful tool for conversations with colleagues, parents, other professionals, and children in our setting.

The round table discussion

This is a forum to which we bring areas of our practice that are associated with the equalities legislation, as well as other pertinent changes to legislation that we particularly need to pay attention to in our school. We have discussed gender issues, female circumcision, issues of sexual identity (LGBTQIA), beliefs, community, culture, issues regarding community cohesion, race, and unconscious bias. We have dealt with various stereotypes as a round table talk; for instance, some of the issues we have addressed over the years include statements such as "All Muslims are terrorists"; "Black people are aggressive and scary"; "All people are born Muslims and have strayed if they are Christians"; "White people are not allowed special treatment in their own country"; "A whites-only group would be frowned upon"; "My religion says homosexuality is wrong"; "Domestic abuse only happens in certain communities"; "Travellers and Gypsies are dirty." In some cases, we do not come away with a solution, but we have a better understanding of where someone is coming from and why they hold these opinions and how they need to manage them in an educational setting. You might baulk at hearing some of these opinions being dealt with openly, but we are mindful that no one is highlighted, so round table discussion topics are placed anonymously in a box and pulled out for discussion. What is interesting is that over the years, as staff become comfortable with each other, every now and then someone will say "That is my question/comment."

The 360-degree questionnaire

This is a team exercise where you rate yourself and the team rates you. The team sits together to carry out this exercise at an appointed time, but it is all done anonymously and handed in to the co-ordinator of the activity. The questionnaire can be adapted to whatever situations need to be dealt with. The data is collated and fed back to individuals, so they understand how they perceive themselves and how others perceive them. Team leaders or the senior leadership team also fill in a questionnaire – no one is exempt. If there are surprising anomalies, development points, or someone is upset, this is addressed using a coaching approach. I have to say that this exercise works in our setting because we have achieved a good level of maturity as a team; most of our staff have been there for over 15 years. An exercise like this needs lead-in time to prepare staff to give and receive feedback.

These exercises are not a cure-all solution for anti-racist practice, nor are they exercises that can be picked out to "fix" people. They have to be conducted as part of the vision that we build within our settings, without individual people feeling singled out or targeted; this can still happen if someone feels particularly sensitive about the areas being addressed, but when we adhere to the rules that we have all helped to design for how these exercises are conducted, these issues usually resolve themselves. This also means that it is good practice to revisit the rules every time, before conducting the exercises, to ensure that everyone is ok with them.

THE SPACE FOR STRUCTURAL CHANGE – VISIBLE

Questions for reflection:

1   Our work schedule is tight. How can we create space and time for "safe space" exercises?
2   Do an audit of the resources in the setting. Are they culturally representative? Do they stereotype people of other cultures? Are our displays inclusive?
3   If funding is low, in what other ways can we acquire inclusive resources within our settings?
4   How will we manage parents or stakeholders who are not happy with developing anti-racist practice in the setting?

Conclusion

Anti-racist practice in the early years entails us as leaders and practitioners staying focused on the preservation of children's rights and having a better understanding of democratic principles, citizenship, and the conscious and unconscious biases that permeate our practice to the continued detriment of black and ethnic minority children. This book offers a philosophical framework to develop exemplary anti-racist policies and practices in early years education. The deeper problem we face is the pervasiveness of systemic racism which has become entangled with how normal everyday citizens, who sometimes do not perceive themselves as "racist" or "privileged," benefit from a post-colonial system that automatically and functionally disenfranchises ethnic minorities. Having that challenged is usually an uncomfortable and emotive experience, but a necessary one for the wellbeing of all children in the early years and beyond.

Humankind is progressing in leaps and bounds in many spheres; however, systemic oppression is rife, and although these issues do not solely affect black and ethnic minority communities, these communities are adversely affected as a matter of course. "The Water of Systems Change" reminds us to never underestimate the invisible; an aspect of the invisible is that we might want to do the best for all children but not really want things to change too much. It is possible that parts of this journey towards anti-racist practice feel like those days when we wake up and just don't want to go in to work, even though we love our jobs; but we drag our feet a bit, muddle through, and soldier on, and by mid-morning we suddenly realise that we have totally forgotten that we hadn't wanted to come in at all that day.

I have one last question to ask. If we woke up tomorrow and the lives of black children and black colleagues mattered just as much as the lives of white children and white colleagues, how would you *truly* feel about that?

DOI: 10.4324/9781003247807-8

Because, in all honesty, these are the thoughts that have to come to the surface to be muddled through to get to a place of true anti-racist practice in the early years. Oluo (2018) encourages us to stop worrying about needing to look inwards to face ourselves when working with anti-racist practice:

> you should instead fear unexamined racism. Fear the thought that right now, you could be contributing to the oppression of others and you don't know it. But do not fear those who bring that oppression to light. Do not fear the opportunity to do better.

(p. 224)

All of us need to constantly look inwards when working with young children, especially as choosing this awesome career should mean that we never give up on trying to do better for the children in our care. Thank you for sticking with me to the end of this journey; the car is a little worse for wear and we are all tired and ready for a long refreshing drink, a soothing bath, and to enjoy some quiet time. Some people are leaving the resort earlier than others and some are leaving later than others but hopefully everyone feels confident enough to drive and navigate their own journey back home. Thank God for mobile phones and vehicle recovery services: we know that even if we break down, we will make it home, with a little help from our friends.

References

Albert, A. (2021) Racism in Nurseries: 'Black Babies Hardly Picked Up and Left in Dirty Nappies for Hours'. daynurseries.co.uk. https://www.daynurseries.co.uk/news/article.cfm/id/1652649/Black-lives-matter-and-children-suffer-racism

Anderson, K. L. (2020). *From Racist to Non-Racist to Anti-Racist: Becoming a Part of the Solution.* Boise State Pressbooks. https://boisestate.pressbooks.pub/antiracist/

Beaumont, J. (1871). *The New Slavery: An Account of the Indian and Chinese Immigrants in British Guiana.* London: W. Ridgway.

Boakye, J. (2022). *I Heard What You Said.* London: Picador Publishing Company.

Bronfenbrenner, U. (1979). *The Ecology of Human Development.* Cambridge, MA: Harvard University Press.

Carmichael, S. and Hamilton, C. (1967). *Black Power: The Politics of Liberation.* New York: Vintage.

Cerdeña, J. P., Plaisime, M. V., & Tsai, J. (2020). From Race-Based to Race-Conscious Medicine: How Anti-Racist Uprisings Call Us to Act. *Lancet,* 396(10257), 1125–1128. https://doi.org/10.1016/s0140-6736(20)32076-6

Coard, B. (1971) *How the West Indian Child Is Made Educationally Subnormal in the British School System: The Scandal of the Black Child in Schools in Britain.* London: New Beacon Books.

Commission on Race and Ethnic Disparities. (2021). *Commission on Race and Ethnic Disparities: The Report.* Cabinet Office, Government UK.

Demie, F., & McLean, C. (2017). *Narrowing the Achievement Gap of Disadvantaged Pupils.* Research and Statistics Unit, Lambeth LA.

Development Education Centre (1986) *Behind the Scenes: Photographs and In-Service Activities for Exploring the Hidden Curriculum.* Birmingham: Development Education Centre.

Durand, M, (2013) The OECD Better Life Initiative: How's Life? And the Measurement of Well-Being. *The Review of Income and Wealth,* (61), 4–17. https://doi.org/10.1111/roiw.12156

Epstein, D. (1993). Too Small to Notice? Constructions of Childhood and Discourses of 'Race' in Predominantly White Contexts. *Curriculum Studies,* 1(3), 317–334. https://doi.org/10.1080/0965975930010302

Fowler, N. (2020). Britain's Slave Owner Compensation Loan, Reparations and Tax Havenry. *Tax Justice Network.* https://taxjustice.net/2020/06/09/slavery-compensation-uk-questions/

Gokhale, G. K. (1912). *Speech Calling for Suspension of Indian Indentured Emigration: Government of India, Legislative Department, Proceedings of the Council of Government.*

https://www.britannica.com/science/information-theory/Physiology

https://www.daynurseries.co.uk/news/article.cfm/id/1652649/Black-lives-matter-and-children-suffer-racism

https://www.independent.co.uk/voices/school-racism-black-students-exclusions-hair-kiss-teeth-a9280296.html

https://www.theguardian.com/world/2020/mar/11/uk-more-nostalgic-for-empire-than-other-ex-colonial-powers

https://www.illinoiscivics.org/standards/anti-racist-classrooms/

Jones, C. P. J. (2000). Levels of Racism: A Theoretic Framework and a Gardener's Tale. *American Journal of Public Health,* 90(8), 1212–1215.

Kania, J., Kramer, M. R., & Senge, P. (2018). *The Water of Systems Change.* Report, Foundation Strategy Group.

Kempadoo, K. (2017). 'Bound Coolies' and Other Indentured Workers in the Caribbean: Implications for Debates about Human Trafficking and Modern Slavery. *Anti-Trafficking Review*, (9), 48–63. www.antitraffickingreview.org

Kendi, I. (2019). *How to Be an Antiracist*. New York: One World.

Kuklinski, M. R., & Weinstein, R. S. (2001). Classroom and developmental differences in a path model of teacher expectancy effects. *Child Development*, *72*(5), 1554–1578. https://doi.org/10.1111/1467-8624.00365

Malaguzzi, L. (1997). quoted in Penn, H., *Comparing Nurseries: Staff and Children in Italy*. Spain and the UK: Paul Chapman Publishing.

Mann, T. C., & Ferguson, M. J. (2015). Can We Undo Our First Impressions? The Role of Reinterpretation in Reversing Implicit Evaluations. *Journal of Personality and Social Psychology*, 108(6), 823–849. https://doi.org/10.1037/pspa0000021

Marmot, M. (2010). *Fair Society, Healthy Lives: The Marmot Review*. Strategic Review of Health Inequalities in England Post-2010. Institute of Health Equity.

Oldfield, J. (2021). Abolition of the Slave Trade and Slavery in Britain. The British Library. https://www.bl.uk/restoration-18th-century-literature/articles/abolition-of-the-slave-trade-and-slavery-in-britain

Oluo, I. (2018). *So You Want to Talk about Race*. New York: Seal Press.

Piaget, J. (1971). The Theory of Stages in Cognitive Development. In D. Green, M. P. Ford, & G. B. Flamer (Eds.), *Measurement and Piaget*. McGraw-Hill (pp. 1–11).

Santayana, G. (1905). *The Life of Reason*. From the series Great Ideas of Western Man: Vol. 1, Ch. 12.

Schlieber, M., & Mclean, C. (2020). *Educator Work Environments Are Children's Learning Environments: How and Why They Should Be Improved*. Center for the Study of Child Care Employment. https://cscce.berkeley.edu/educatorwork-environments-are-childrens-learning-environments-how-and-why-they-should-be-improved/

Shand-Baptiste, K. (2020). UK Schools Have Targeted Black Children for Generations. *The Independent.* https://www.independent.co .uk/voices/school-racism-black-students-exclusions-hair-kiss-teeth -a9280296.html

Tolle, E. (2004). *The Power of Now: A Guide to Spiritual Enlightenment.* Sydney: Hachette New World Library.

Van Yperen, N. W., & Buunk, B. P. (1991). Sex-Role Attitudes, Social Comparison, and Satisfaction with Relationships. *Social Psychology Quarterly,* 54(2), 169–180.

Vincent, C., Rollock, N., Ball, S., & Gillborn, D. (2012). The Educational Strategies of the Black Middle Classes. In *The Politicization of Parenthood* (pp. 139–152). https://doi.org/10.1007/978-94-007 -2972-8_11

Wilkinson, R., & Pickett, K. (2009). *The Spirit Level: Why More Equal Societies Almost Always Do Better.* London: Allen Lane.

World Bank Annual Report. (2013). End Extreme Poverty, Promote Shared Prosperity. World Bank. https://openknowledge.worldbank .org/bitstream/handle/10986/16091/9780821399378.pdf?sequence =1&isAllowed=y

Index